Celebrating Creation

Affirming Catholicism and the Revelation of God's Glory

Edited by
MARK D. CHAPMAN

DARTON·LONGMAN + TODD

First published in 2004 by
Darton, Longman and Todd Ltd
1 Spencer Court
140-142 Wandsworth High Street
London SW18 4JJ

ISBN 0-232-52560-9

A catalogue record for this book is available from the British Library.

Phototypeset by Intype Libra Ltd
Printed and bound in Great Britain by
Page Bros, Norwich, Norfolk

Celebrating Creation

Frank,

A wonderfull book —
I love you very.

Love,

Contents

Acknowledgements

Thanks are due to Lisa Martell, administrator of Affirming Catholicism, and to Martin Lawrence and the planning group, for their energy and commitment in organising the conference, and also to the staff of St Chad's College, Durham, particularly the highly efficient conference manager, James Randle for helping to make it such a happy occasion. Without them there would have been no conference and no book. I am also grateful to Sophie Farrant for her assistance in transcribing John Gaskell's lecture. The citations from *Miss Garnet's Angel* are reprinted with permission of HarperCollins Publishers Ltd © Salley Vickers, 2000. The citation from John Betjeman, 'In a Bath Tea Shop' is reproduced by permission of John Murray (Publishers).

Mark D. Chapman
Epiphany 2004

Notes on Contributors

DAVID BROWN is Van Mildert Professor of Divinity in the University of Durham and Canon Librarian of Durham Cathedral.

MARK CHAPMAN is Vice-Principal of Ripon College ,Cuddesdon and a member of the faculty of Theology at Oxford University. He is publications officer for Affirming Catholicism.

JOHN GASKELL is honorary assistant priest at All Saints', Margaret Street, London. Previously he was vicar of St Alban's, Holborn, and was until recently chair of the trustees of Affirming Catholicism.

MICHAEL HEMPEL is Senior Tutor and Director of Development at St Chad's College, Durham. He is researching on religious drama of the 1930s. Previously he was precentor of Durham Cathedral.

JEFFREY JOHN is Canon Theologian and Chancellor of Southwark Cathedral. He was appointed Bishop of Reading in the summer of 2003 but did not take up the post. He was appointed Dean of St Albans in 2004. He is a founder member and trustee of Affirming Catholicism.

JACK NICHOLLS is Bishop of Sheffield. He was previously Bishop of Lancaster. His best friend in heaven is St Seraphim of Sarov.

MARK OAKLEY is Rector of St Paul's, Covent Garden and

Deputy Priest-in-Ordinary to the Queen. He is the author of *The Collage of God* (DLT, 2001).

BRENDAN O'MALLEY is Dean of Chapel and part-time lecturer at the University of Wales, Lampeter. A former Cistercian monk he has written widely on Celtic spirituality.

VICTOR STOCK is Dean of Guildford Cathedral. Previously he was Rector of St Mary-le-Bow. He was a founder member of Affirming Catholicism.

ANGELA TILBY is Vice-Principal of Westcott House and is writing a book on contemporary spirituality. Previously she worked as a producer in radio and television.

KATE TRISTRAM is Curate of Lindisfarne and has been Warden of Marygate House. She is currently researching the writings of Columbanus. Previously she was Head of Religious Studies at the College of St Hild and St Bede, Durham.

FRASER WATTS is Starbridge Lecturer in Theology and Natural Sciences in the University of Cambridge and Fellow of Queen's College. He is Director of the Psychology and Religion Research Programme in the Centre for Advanced Religious and Theological Studies.

Introduction: Celebrating Creation

Mark D. Chapman

The Church and the World

The summer of 2003 was not a happy time for the Church of England, nor for the Anglican Communion more generally. Issues of sex and sexuality, which had never been far from the surface, threatened to tear the church to pieces. While the actual discussions often appeared in the guise of methods of biblical interpretation, the debate was usually focused on the relationship of the church and the world – over the summer of 2003 it soon became clear that within the Church of England, and even more obviously within the Anglican Communion, there are quite different ways of understanding God's relationship with the world. For some Christians, the church is set against the world. Its standards are quite distinct from those outside. It has its clear ethical and doctrinal boundaries and it should resist the evils of secularity, with its rationalism, consumerism, hedonism and immorality, as forcefully as possible. The world may have been created good but it soon fell from grace to such an extent that it could reveal nothing about God; God's kingdom is not of this world.[1] Boundary markers, ethical distinctiveness and doctrinal clarity, based on a literalistic interpretation of Scripture, characterise such Christians, whose missionary goal is to evangelise a fallen world.[2]

For other Christians, however, the world is created good and still reflects something of the glory of its creator. And that is quite simply because God chose to dwell in that world – while it might have gone its own way and departed from God's will, it is nevertheless still the same world

1

that was redeemed by God through his incarnate son. It is through the worldly substance of the flesh that God's glory is revealed in Christ. Consequently the boundaries between God and the world are not hard and fast. As Angela Tilby puts it in her essay in this volume, the world is God's 'primary sacrament', where something of God's true nature and glory is revealed. The tension between these two understandings of God's relationship with the world is well expressed by the great nineteenth-century theologian, F. D. Maurice, with more than a hint of irony: 'The Father loves the world, the Son dies for the world, the Holy Ghost convinces the world that it has a Deliverer and a Righteous Lord, and that he has taken it out of the hands of a usurper; and the Church, which is sealed with his name, is not to love the world, not to save the world, not to convince the world, but to set itself up as a rival competitor to the world, to plot against the world, to undermine the world!'[3] It is perhaps reassuring to know that the contemporary crisis in the Anglican Communion is far from new.

For so many in the catholic tradition of Anglicanism, God has been glimpsed through the world he created. God does not remain aloof in some ethereal sphere out of contact with the world, but voluntarily chooses to dwell in this world. That is why the world can be seen as God's primary sacrament. In the 150th anniversary of the birth of one of the great founder figures of liberal catholicism, Charles Gore (1853–1932), it is important to recall the central importance of the incarnation. For Gore, God chose to limit himself in order to dwell in creation as an expression of his super-abundant love for the world: the world was structured on love and not punishment. Thus the Son abandons 'the divine mode of his existence' for the sake of the love of his creation.[4] It is this principle of God's voluntary self-emptying, which has been called kenosis, that lies at the basis of the Anglican doctrine of the incarnation. The material and the physical are not to be regarded as lower aspects of Christ, but are necessary for Christ to be both God and a human being, for God truly to love the world he made; the material and the physical were the form in which God's love was revealed. God loves us, even trusts us, so much that he has to learn how to be a human at his mother's knee, as Max Ernst's great painting of the Virgin Mary chastising her infant son, discussed below by David Brown, brilliantly demonstrates. Consequently, Christianity is not to be lived in a strange spiritual world separated off from the material world, but instead it is precisely in the material and natural world that God is to be found: 'In great measure,' Gore wrote, 'the self-sacrifice of the Incarnation seems to have lain in [Christ's] refraining from the exercise of what he possessed, or from the divine mode of action, that he might live under conditions of true manhood.'[5] That, perhaps, is the greatest challenge to those forms of Christianity which deny the capacity for God's beauty and glory to be revealed in creation.

Celebrating Creation is an attempt to breathe new life into this threatened incarnational tradition and for that reason it is a book that challenges the virtual dualism of so much recent theological discussion. It emphasises the joyfulness of being human, the difficulty of separating the saint from the sinner, and asks us once again to search the human and the natural worlds for glimpses of God's beauty and glory. And it may well be that there will be far more beauty and glory in these worlds of God's creation than in the church itself, which so often seems devoted to a gospel of exclusion, condemnation and separation. God's love is certainly not the preserve of the church, but is visible in our world which has been embraced by the same God who embraced our worldly flesh. Indeed love, longing and struggle may be far more clearly perceived in the world as it comes to birth in all its triumphant diversity. This is the love expressed in the Eucharist, the sacrament of unity, in which all share in the gratitude for life itself. But it is a unity expressed in a human and natural diversity and even disorder without clear-cut boundaries and without the simplicity of certainty. God emptied himself to reveal himself: from that time onwards Christianity has been a religion of the search, the unknown, the experimental and of longing. And that is a search through all the resources we have – most obviously, Scripture and tradition, but also life itself, where God chose to display his questioning presence. The essays in this book do not supply answers but take us on an experimental journey as we become searchers on a path towards understanding that questioning presence. Some Anglican catholics are proud of the fact that they do not know the answers since in the light of the incarnation there simply cannot be any answers. Yet it is by asking the questions that the world might be seen to be redeemed. Such questions, however, seemed very distant in the summer of 2003.

Affirming Catholicism and the Summer of 2003

Following the announcement on 20 May that Dr Jeffrey John, Chancellor of Southwark Cathedral, was to be appointed Bishop of Reading, there followed what can only be described as an extraordinary and at times shocking chain of events. There were letters, petitions, responses and counter-petitions; new websites were set up for those opposed to practising gay clergy and those in favour of an 'inclusive church'; extraordinary passion and anger were unleashed on both sides.[6] Indeed, the Church of England was in the national news almost daily, and things grew even more intense when it was announced that the Diocese of New Hampshire was set to consecrate an open and practising homosexual as bishop. A little local difficulty in the Berkshire archdeaconry had become part of a global issue which appeared to threaten the fragile unity of the Anglican Communion.

Perhaps the most surprising thing of all for the Church of England, however, was that the doctrine of episcopal collegiality was openly challenged from among the bishops themselves. The doctrine of collegiality – which was in reality little more than a pragmatic fudge to create a semblance of unity over the ordination of women, principally to paper over the diametrically opposed opinions of bishops – broke down over the issue of same-sex relationships. This time, a number of bishops refused to compromise. In a letter to the *Church Times* nine English diocesan bishops[7] supported by seven suffragans[8] from all wings of the church were prepared to break ranks and openly challenge the judgement of one of their peers (as well as the authority of the Crown which officially made the appointment). In writing their letter they hoped to 'give encouragement to clergy and laity of orthodox persuasion that many bishops share their serious concern, and to do so without making any threats or demands'. The final clause was of course a nonsense – the threat was scarcely veiled and the battle lines were evidently being drawn. But even more disturbing was the fact that, almost certainly for the first time in the history of the Church of England, the issue of same-sex relationships was elevated into a test of what counted as the 'orthodox persuasion'. Orthodoxy was no longer a matter of assent to the catholic creeds, but instead demanded belief in sexual intercourse within marriage as the only legitimate sphere for sexual activity. Evident anger led to extraordinarily immoderate and illiberal language: lack of orthodoxy (or heresy) is, after all, grounds for breaking communion.

The grounds for the bishops' challenge to Dr John's appointment did not come directly from the few problematic passages of Scripture about same-sex relationships (or acts) but from an understanding of what they called the 'complementarity' of men and women, which they regarded as part of 'the order of Creation'. It was all very simple: God intended marriage to be between men and women and in consequence, 'Sexual intercourse within the life-long relationship of marriage is the sign and beautiful expression of that union. Intercourse outside marriage undermines the power of that sign.' To practise any other form of sexual relationship is to contravene the order of creation and thus to work against the will of God for the world. This natural law argument is straightforward and has been rehearsed by many others. It is well summarised in the recent discussion document *Some Issues in Human Sexuality.*[9] A similar argument (but with a greater emphasis on the Fall) was also used in the influential 1997 Kuala Lumpur Statement of conservative Anglicans from the global south.[10]

The nine English bishops did not stop with a simple re-affirmation of traditional teaching, but went considerably further in ruling out the freedom of church leaders to challenge this teaching. Indeed it was his advocacy of the permissibility of committed same-sex partnerships with a sexual expression that proved sufficient grounds to oppose Jeffrey John's appointment. For the bishops, it was impossible even to contemplate alternatives to sex within marriage, simply because God had willed all sexual relationships to be of one kind. Their charge against Jeffrey John was what they called his 'severe criticism of orthodox teaching' in his 1993 Affirming Catholicism booklet 'Permanent, Faithful, Stable'.[11] Despite his unambiguous statement that as a bishop he would abide by the Church's current statement on the status of same-sex partnerships (Issues in Human Sexuality),[12] and although he publicly declared that his relationship had long been celibate,[13] the bishops opposed his appointment, voicing their 'concern because of the Church's constant teaching, in the light of Scripture and because of the basic ordering of men and women in creation. We must also express our concern because of our responsibility for the Church's unity, both in this country and throughout the world.' The second pragmatic ground might eventually have won the day, but the wider implications of the bishops' letter should not be underestimated. Sexual relations between members of the same sex are always disordered and work against God's creation; and even to think differently opens one up to the charge of heresy (or lack of an 'orthodox persuasion'). If nothing else, the bishops' letter was at least clear and unambiguous.

For members and supporters of Affirming Catholicism this challenge to Jeffrey John's appointment as Bishop of Reading came as a bitter blow, especially after he was eventually persuaded to withdraw from the post on 6 July. He was, after all, a founder and trustee of the movement and he has continued to be an enthusiastic supporter. Furthermore, his 'heretical' booklet was produced in the Affirming Catholicism series, which seeks to promote open discussion and debate. For those who knew him there was obviously a great deal of personal sympathy – a prurient and intrusive press (and church) meant that he had been forced to reveal more about his private life than should be expected of anybody. Not surprisingly there was much deeply felt anger among his supporters, such as that voiced by Colin Slee, Dean of Southwark, in his announcement of Jeffrey John's withdrawal during the Sunday Eucharist in his cathedral:

The news will hurt thousands of Christian people who are not gay but believe strongly in God's love and redemption for all his children equally. It is irrelevant to God's love whether people are male or female, slave or free, black or white, gay or heterosexual. We are addressing spiritual apartheid . . . In the peace marches earlier this year the slogan 'Not in my name' was used to great effect. Let me say very clearly that this action is certainly not in my name and I am bound to say I find it very hard to see how it can conceivably be seen to be in God's name.

While most responses were more guarded, there was nevertheless a very real sense in which many felt that the Church of England had lost a man who possessed a great deal of pastoral wisdom and insight together with a very real sense of mission, and who would have made a fine bishop. His simple reflections on the seven last words of Christ on the cross included in this volume bear adequate witness to these gifts. There was deep sorrow for Jeffrey John, but also for Archbishop Rowan Williams, another founder member of Affirming Catholicism, as he struggled to maintain unity in a church in which the same controversies were echoed at a global level but complicated still further by the huge cultural differences separating the different provinces. For many, however, the anger moved beyond this personal sadness: the very idea of a church that might respond to new insights and challenges by opening itself up to the world seemed to have been lost, to be replaced by a church forever tied to the bigotry and prejudices of a distant past.

At the same time, there was obviously a huge underestimation on the part of those responsible for Jeffrey John's appointment of the vociferousness of the opposition. It soon became clear that many sincere and intelligent people who had been quite prepared to accept re-interpretation of Scripture on such matters as the role of women in ministry, and the permissibility of contraception (where, incidentally, very similar arguments from the 'natural order' of creation are still used by the Roman Catholic Church against its practice) and divorce, saw homosexual relations, particularly among the clergy, as of a quite different order. The acceptability of homosexual sexual activity was elevated into a test of the boundaries of permissible belief. There was a clamour for clarity, as had been noted in the Kuala Lumpur Statement: 'We believe that the clear and unambiguous teaching of the Holy Scriptures about human sexuality is of great help to Christians as it provides clear boundaries.' Two lecturers at Wycliffe Hall, an Evangelical Anglican college in Oxford, summarised the position well in a letter from an organisation called Anglican Mainstream to the *Church of England Newspaper*. They claimed that Jeffrey John's

> recent statements show the confusion he will create when he uses his teaching office to undermine the common mind of the House of Bishops. Of course, other bishops do not agree with *Issues [in Human Sexuality]* but there has been collective responsibility until now. To consecrate so vocal a critic and allow him to speak out publicly is a novelty already undoing recent hard-won gains in church discussion . . . Many orthodox believers see a clear line in the sand here and are determined to speak and, if necessary, act together against this nomination.[14]

A loyal and devout Anglican was thus made a scapegoat in the question of identity-formation, which has always been a great fixation of church parties. Boundaries of identity were being established over homosexuality and especially the issue of homosexual ordination, just as some years before they had been set up (usually by Anglo-Catholics) over the unacceptability of women's ordination. Indeed the parallels are striking – once again issues of sexual identity were couched in terms of theological opinion and doctrinal orthodoxy. Similarly, there have been calls over both issues for a doctrinally and ethically pure church untainted by bishops who challenge the teachings which the group believes to be badges of doctrinal orthodoxy. The writers of the Anglican Mainstream letter looked 'to explore non-geographical forms of episcopacy to serve a post-Christendom missionary church'.

What Was There to Celebrate?

Not surprisingly, many of us travelled to Durham for the conference, *Celebrating Creation*, with a heavy heart, unsure of whether we wanted to have anything to do with a church which was so obviously tearing itself to pieces over issues which must have seemed utterly incredulous to so many in the world outside and even to many within the church. Racism might no longer be acceptable in the church but sexism and homophobia – and even the lack of toleration of freedom of speech about the ethics of sexual relationships – still seemed to be quite permissible, however much the cry was made to the contrary. As a priest of the diocese of Oxford I caught the train to Durham wondering what the world outside could now make of the Bishop of Oxford's remarks to his diocesan synod:

> I want a diocese that is able to show everyone, including gay and lesbian people, that they are beloved of God. Are the gay and lesbian people in our churches, of whom there are a good many, able to feel fully accepted by God and their fellow Christians, or are they riven by feelings of self-hatred? When our fellow Christians stand before God, do they think of themselves as an accident, a freak, or deeply loved? And if we want them to feel deeply loved, are our present attitudes as a Church helping or hindering? When our Christian sisters and brothers say, 'Who am I before you, O God?', what answer do they hear from us? This is a spiritual issue, a gospel issue.[15]

Like many others I struggled through the summer of 2003, finding it difficult to preach about the God of mercy and the God of love in a church so obviously expressing hatred. Sexual relationships which I was sure could express something of the beauty of God's covenant with the world, were always disordered. Sex within marriage, on the other hand, was 'beautiful'. Selective silence seemed to apply: it was amazing that nobody spoke of the levels of violence and abuse that often accompany sexual intercourse within marriage. But, as the Archbishop of Sydney, Peter Jensen, put it, 'Our Creator does have a view on sex and the expression of sexuality,' and that is the Creator who

> created men and women and blessed them in life-long, heterosexual marriage. So important is the positive teaching that it is reinforced by the negatives against all other forms of sexual activity outside this norm. This has always been the plain meaning and reading of the Scripture and the historic understanding of

the Christian church. This teaching is stated positively in the opening chapters of the book of Genesis. It is reaffirmed in the teaching of Jesus who specifically endorsed the statements of those opening chapters. It is stated negatively in Jesus' strong words about those who break up marriages. When the apostle Paul brought the message of God to the non-Jewish world, various ritual and ceremonial practices were abolished, but not the teaching related to marriage and sexual practices.[16]

Like the bishops' letter, Archbishop Jensen's response made use of the doctrine of creation to deny the acceptability of same-sex relationships. There consequently seemed to be something sadly ironic in the theme of the Affirming Catholicism conference, *Celebrating Creation*. God's creation appeared to be unjust and arbitrary – and men and women created by God, yet not attracted to members of the opposite sex, were somehow misfits and disordered. Or, as some have suggested, they were simply forced into homosexuality by their cultural circumstances and could be 'cured' given changed conditions. Others felt that homosexuals had simply made a lifestyle choice.

Many of us brought a number of far-reaching questions with us to Durham. God could easily look like a tyrant in creating these strange and disordered people forever forced to accept their lot of celibacy and see the world of heterosexual marriage as normal. If that was the case, then what could there be to celebrate in creation for gay people who chose to express their love for one another physically? And what was left for the rest of us to celebrate other than giving thanks, like the Pharisee, that we were lucky enough to be attracted to members of the opposite sex, and fortunate enough not to be destined for a life either of celibacy or of disordered relationships which contradicted the laws of creation?

The Joy of Creation

With so much bitterness and anger, a conference on *Celebrating Creation* had the potential to become a wake for liberal-minded catholicism, a celebration of the death of an experiment with secularity which had failed through compromise and which was being supplanted by forces deeply hostile to the world outside the church. But the good news is that it wasn't like that. From the very start there was an air of celebration – a celebration of a God who could be found in the most unlikely places; a God who was a God of laughter as well as tears; a God who worked through sinners as well as saints. There was a need to laugh together – to discover a sense of joy despite the pain. Catholics have so often been criticised for their up-tight spirituality reserved for the religious athlete, but for these Anglican catholics who spent a few days in Durham it was important not to revel in escapist and pious devotion, but to celebrate God's goodness in all his creation.

And with that joy came a playfulness and a cheerfulness which began to put things into perspective. Whatever else was going on in the church, the incarnation was still true: the Son of Man ate with tax collectors and sinners and yet the religious zealots of his own time called him a glutton and a drunkard. Is that perhaps because he had a good time and refused to be sucked into the navel-gazing religion of his sectarian contemporaries? Is that because he enjoyed the company of those who made him think differently? Now playfulness and cheerfulness may not be the great cardinal virtues, but they seem to me to be at the heart of the message of the man who so often wore his religion lightly (and who wasn't afraid of destroying the occasional temple). Our God was a God who feasted with sinners and opened himself to strangers and outsiders and those who disagreed with him – he emptied himself to be one of us; he didn't simply do what the books of the law – even the so-called 'natural law' – taught him. Perhaps he was with sinners for sheer pleasure, simply because they were fun to be with, and perhaps that is how he learnt to see life anew and to redirect his priorities away from religion towards the Kingdom of God. That was God's way of inclusiveness which came as a great contrast to the anger and the bitterness of the summer months.

The laughter in the bar at St Chad's College, Durham reaffirmed many in their faith – there was still something to celebrate in creation after all; even in those bits which don't usually contribute to what we might call spirituality. And this set the theme for the conference. In their different ways all the speakers experimented with the playfulness of a God who displays his glory and his beauty often in the most unlikely places. As any blues guitar player knows, the devil has all the best tunes, but those are the same tunes that teach us about God, even though they are the tunes condemned without a hearing by so many of those who seek to define orthodoxy. *Celebrating Creation* was a conference – and has become a book – in which the boundaries between the world and the church have collapsed and where God is seen to be speaking through the sinner as well as in the saint. As the authors emphasise, there is much to learn from pagans, even when there is so often a reluctance on the part of Christians to listen to those with a different view of the world – but it is precisely from those who are different, but still made in the image of their creator, from whom we so often learn new things about God.

Durham Cathedral itself gave us an extraordinary resource to reflect on creation, as Victor Stock reminded us as he took the conference on a prayer tour through the majesty of the building. He challenged many of us to think again about the role of cathedrals and their inclusive mission as beacons of the divine. His capacity to mingle laughter with tears – surely the mark of the true Christian spirituality – will not be forgotten quickly (not least by the Dean of Durham). A symbol of Norman oppression and power which said much about the political circumstances of the time of its construction, was at one and the same time a building which spoke eloquently of God's transcendence and human creativity. Throughout the Conference the presence of the mighty Cathedral meant that it was impossible to separate the world and the church, even if the stewards of the cathedral did their best to keep visitors out by barring off the nave during our services.

One lecture has not been reproduced in this volume quite simply because it is impossible to put into words the guided tour of the Durham peninsula by the great naturalist, Professor David Bellamy, who has lived on the peninsula for years and who loves the city of Durham with a passion that could be matched by few. A crowd of people admiring the beauty of the tiny plant expounded by a great enthusiast for God's good earth was an experience that simply does not transfer to the written page. But both the experience of the cathedral and the peninsula, as well as the great beauty of the worship in St Oswald's, allowed us to celebrate where celebration had earlier seemed so inappropriate.

So in the end *Celebrating Creation* is a surprisingly optimistic book: it has the air of thanksgiving for the God who made the world and made all of us different. Even though we might all fall short of the glory of God, still we can reveal something of that glory – despite our shortcomings the God who became one of us still loves us. That is the simple inclusivity for which Affirming Catholicism stands and which all of us who are involved in the movement sincerely hope will survive into the future. But if it doesn't, God may still reveal his glory somewhere quite unexpected – after all, he has done it before. We have no reason to worry.

Notes

1 John 18:36.

2 A good, if somewhat extreme, example of this form of Christianity, is that maintained by the Anglican group Reform. See www.reform.org.uk/covenant.

3 F. D. Maurice, *Lincoln's Inn Sermons* (London: Macmillan, 6 vols, 1891–2), here vol. 1, p. 249.

4 Charles Gore, *Dissertations on Subjects Connected with the Incarnation* (London: John Murray, 1895). Gore maintains this theory consistently through his life. See, for instance, *Can We Then Believe?* (London: John Murray, 1926), p. 194.

5 Gore, *The Incarnation of the Son of God* (London: John Murray, 1891), pp. 265–6.

6 Anglican Mainstream, an umbrella organisation of conservative Anglicans, even set up a special Bishop of Reading website where nearly all the relevant material has been posted: www.bishop-reading.org.uk. A number of concerned liberals set up www.inclusivechurch.net.

7 Letter of 16 June 2003 to the *Church Times* from the Bishops of Bradford, Carlisle, Chester, Chichester, Exeter, Liverpool, Rochester, Southwell and Winchester.

8 The suffragan bishops were those of Bedford, Bolton, Lewes, Maidstone, Penrith, Tewkesbury and Willesden.

9 *Some Issues in Human Sexuality* (London: Church House Publishing, 2003), §§ 3.4.51–114.

10 For the Kuala Lumpur statement see
www.reform.org.uk/bb/-kuala.html.

11 *'Permanent, Faithful, Stable'*, new edition (London: Darton, Longman and Todd, 2000).

12 *Issues in Human Sexuality: a Statement by the House of Bishops of the General Synod of the Church of England* (London: Church House Publishing, 1991).

13 This was made unambiguously in the *Guardian* on 20 June 2003.

14 3 July 2003, posted at www.anglican-mainstream.net/news1.htm. The letter was written by Andrew Goddard and Peter Walker.

15 Press release of 9 June 2003 at
www.oxford.anglican.org/-detail.php?id=435.

16 Open letter to Peter Carnley, the Australian Primate, 2 July 2003 at www.anglicancommunion.org/acns/articles/34/75/acns3494.html.

1 The Glory of God Revealed in Creation

Angela Tilby

Creation in the Anglican Tradition

I am very glad that our theme at this conference is *The Glory of God in Creation*. It is both a Catholic theme and, more specifically, an Anglican theme. The Church of England has been particularly blessed by poets and hymn writers who have treated creation as God's primary sacrament, the outward and visible sign of his graciousness and self-giving. It is no accident that our church has also nurtured amateur and professional botanists and zoologists, not least among the country clergy. The pattern of Morning and Evening Prayer, with its constant rhythmic recitation of the psalms, helps to engender a contemplative perspective on the natural world. It is good to remember that alongside the tedious debates on creation and evolution that followed the publication of Darwin's *Origin of Species* plenty of pious churchmen and women found it was possible to take an unprejudiced interest in natural science, confirming the intuitions of our spiritual tradition that there are links between the rhythm of the seasons and those of the human heart. The poetry of creation in the Anglican tradition has been joyous without usually being sentimental. It has not been unaware of the dark side of the natural world, of cruelty and waste in nature, but there is a balance. A love of season, landscape and place are all familiar parts of our heritage.

Creation in Early Christianity

To see creation as God's primary sacrament is a way of seeing the world which goes back far beyond the formation

15

of the Church of England. It belongs, I believe, to the earliest preaching and teaching of the apostles and their successors, the apostolic fathers and the apologists, who defended the faith in the early centuries of the Roman Empire. I remember being astonished when, as an evangelical nineteen-year-old, beginning to read theology at Cambridge, I discovered that the primitive gospel was not something along the lines of 'Jesus died for your sins and here's an infallible text to prove it' but something more like 'there is one God of heaven and earth and Jesus Christ has made him known'. Jesus Christ has made him known! The identity of the creator, revealed by his Son *was* the new thing, the Good News, as soon as the church began preaching to the Gentiles. You can see that from the preaching ascribed to Paul in the Acts of the Apostles.

The apologists, Justin, Athenagoras and Tertullian develop the theme. There is one God, the creator of heaven and earth, who has made himself known in Jesus Christ. Then it is taken up by perhaps the greatest of the early Christian theologians, Irenaeus of Lyons. Irenaeus and his contemporaries were addressing a world in which most sensitive and thoughtful people found the material universe opaque. They also found aspects of the world, the human body for instance, depressing and distasteful. There is an excitement and tenderness towards the natural world in Irenaeus' writing, a surprising love of the materiality of it, an appreciation of its potential for glory, which is linked to a deep awareness that 'the graciousness of God in Jesus Christ runs seamlessly through the whole of created reality.' For Irenaeus, Christ was the purpose of creation, who summed up or recapitulated God's design in his own person, making God known in a new and definitive way. One of the preferred titles for Jesus in the early Church, until it got lost in the Arian controversy, was that significant phrase from Colossians as 'the first-born of all creation' (Colossians 1:15).

The prevailing philosophy of late antiquity found the idea that God could be *known* by human beings rather vulgar. Christianity came into the world not only making this claim, but also insisting that the birth and death of Jesus of Nazareth was the birth and death and rising again of the

Son of God. Christ was born? How disgusting! He died? How pathetic!

I found it was a profound liberation to realise that the Gospel had this all-embracing and cosmic dimension, that God is, as Irenaeus put it, 'the place of the world'. And that Christ is not God's second best, his last minute rescue plan after the fall, but his first and best gift, because everything is made through the life-giving Logos, through the Word (John 1:3). It helped me to understand that God's generosity is not confined to letting a select few off the punishment for their sins, but is about bringing the whole cosmos to the glory which is its destiny. It helped me to understand that redemption is the fulfilment of creation because God loves what he has made and has declared it good.

It also helped me to recognise that the appropriate response to all this could only be thankfulness. If everything really does come to us as God's gift then my life, *our* life, is already shaped by Eucharist. We are bound to give thanks not only for the specific gifts of creation but also for the fact that our very being is derived from God: 'It is he that hath made us and not we ourselves, we are his people and the sheep of his pasture' (Psalm 100:3). Seen in this light, creation itself must be God's primary sacrament and sign of who he is and what he intends. The consequence of this for us is that it means that the way we conduct ourselves on earth, and the way we behave towards the creatures of the earth is a measure of our capacity to receive the gift.

Creation in Contemporary Culture

How does our contemporary world see nature? I think the answer to that is with both wonder and bafflement. The wonder is obvious in the immense popularity of wildlife television, in the plethora of popular books about astronomy and even in the more mundane celebrations of the natural world in gardening and cookery. Creation is what we are aware of in leisure, in re-creation. But alongside this wonder, there is also another response, bafflement.

I sometimes think that Catholic Christians find themselves in a battlefield between atheists and fundamentalists.

The atheists get access to television and radio and their books sell because both as personalities and as communicators they are plausible and shocking. In this age when few are brought up to read Scripture they are curiously obsessed with the Bible and proving it wrong about creation. They relish the apparent mindlessness of natural processes. They like to heighten the drama of our appalling aloneness in the great cosmos. And then, lined up against them are their enemies and spiritual siblings, the biblical fundamentalists.

Both sides like to read Genesis as though it were a kind of *recipe*. (The wonderful thing about Delia Smith is that if you do exactly what she says you will always get the same result – utterly reliable, utterly foolproof.) If we read the first chapters of Genesis as though they were a recipe you will think of our world as one the great architect has pre-designed for particular species to work in utterly distinctive ways, to reproduce after their kind for ever and ever. The problem fundamentalists have with evolution is that they cannot allow for anything that God has made to become anything else. Any development of creation suggests a God who is not quite as in control as might be desirable, an architect with a quirk who allows the building to respond in some way to its circumstances.

The Disassociation of Sensibility

It was an Eastern Orthodox theologian, John Romanides, who suggested to me that biblical fundamentalism and scientific reductionism were symptoms of the same spiritual sickness which he describes in terms of split or separation. Separation between head and heart, mind and body, text and experience. This sickness is what the poet T. S. Eliot called the 'disassociation of sensibility', and he traced it back to the English Enlightenment. Fundamentalist Christians and reductionist atheists actually inhabit the same sort of universe, on different sides of the same looking glass. It is a clockwork world of cause and effect, running on its neat little tramlines produced by blind nature if you are an atheist, or God if you are a biblical believer.

The split diagnosed by John Romanides and T. S. Eliot is not easily healed. We cannot jump straight into a world where head and heart are integrated. Perhaps there never was such a world. But I am aware of a nostalgia in myself for the medieval vision of the cosmos – that sense of order and grandeur and beauty and delight which you get in Durham Cathedral for example. C. S. Lewis, in his book *The Discarded Image*, describes the medieval universe as something like a great building, dazzling with light and full of the music of the angels. When our ancestors looked up at the night sky they saw much the same as we see, only to them the silence and darkness of what we call space, was simply a consequence of the fact that Earth was cast in permanent shadow. Unlike us, they *knew* that as you ascended into the heavens you would get nearer and nearer to the real world as it poured forth praise to the glory of God.

When we look up at the night sky we first see our own light, the lights of cities and motorways and satellites and planes. And then the random scattered stars, and beyond them the great emptiness of space. Such a cosmos seems cold to us. It makes us agoraphobic. We create artificial light to see where we are. But our light is not the light of revelation, it is the light of enquiry. The inquisitorial light of the lens, whether camera or microscope, is a light that is analytical rather than doxological, and it neither seeks, nor expects to find, anything beyond the material.

So finding the glory of God in creation is not straightforward for us. We live in a world which does not, perhaps cannot, see the glory. And this short-sightedness, this spiritual myopia, is as present in some strands of reformed theology as it is in reductionist science. It is not surprising that the two mirror each other. The reformed doctrine of creation seems to say that we can only know God as creator through Scripture. Our own experience and our reflection on our experience count for nothing. Scriptural theology strips the sacred out of nature and the stage is prepared for the drama of a God who is either the voice of a text or nothing at all. Fundamentalism or atheism – there is no mediating position of the kind which a Catholic theology might allow for. In fact it seems to me that we are being squeezed between a joyless, heartless biblicism, and the kind of atheism that is founded on hatred of the very idea of God. Increasingly, it seems, we are being squeezed out in order

19

for the war between atheists and fundamentalists to take place. Neither side wants to believe that there can be intelligent middle-ground. Each attempts to polarise the other into absurdity. The rampant and uncritical reformed theology which prevails in some parts of the Anglican world is destroying the delicate balance which is the genius of Anglicanism, in which Scripture is interpreted through reason and tradition.

Even among the theologically serious, the Anglican appreciation of creation is undermined by an over-enthusiasm for Calvinist neo-orthodoxy. Nobody could call Karl Barth a fundamentalist but it does shed light on our current problems to know that he found visiting the zoo a deeply unsettling experience. 'What are all these enigmatic creatures of God . . . but so many problems to which we have no answer?' In the whole of the *Church Dogmatics* he never once discussed contemporary cosmology. The reason for this apparent omission is his assumption that knowledge of God as creator must be through revelation alone and that it must be received by faith alone; and such revelation and faith must never be contaminated by being, as he puts it, 'accessible by way of observation or logical thinking'. He abhors natural theology.

Creation and the Worshipping Imagination

Yet I do not think our celebration of the glory of God in creation depends on the kind of natural theology which science has discredited. We cannot now say that nature points unambiguously to God because of the way it is designed, nor that our need for an explanation of nature means that there must be an ultimate explanation in terms of a personal creator. What I think we can say is that God as creator is accessible to the imagination, and particularly to the imagination formed by worship. The Catholic disciplines of meditation, daily office and Eucharist are intended to distance us from our habitual anxieties and ambitions and make us receptive to creation as God's gift and sacrament. Saying the psalms day after day puts us in touch with the exhilaration of being alive in a profoundly ordered, mysterious, beautiful and sometimes terrifying world.

A Catholic theology of creation, then, is derived from worship, and from our response to God as both giver and gift. Creation in the Catholic vision is scriptural, experiential and christocentric. This last point is important. Creation is part of the gospel. It is because of Christ that creation has coherence, because of Christ that we see all things held together in God. This recognition was put into memorable form by St John of Damascus during the first phase of the iconoclastic controversy when the church was divided on the issue of whether it was legitimate to make images of Christ and the saints.

> I make an image of the God whom I see (that is, Jesus). I do not worship matter; I worship the creator of matter who became matter for my sake, who willed to take his abode in matter, who worked out my salvation through matter. Never will I cease honouring the matter which wrought my salvation . . . because of this I salute all matter with reverence, because God has filled it with his grace and power. (*On the Divine Images*, I:16–17)

This material world is open to God's glory, not only because it is derived from God but because it has been taken up into God in the incarnation, the 'creator of matter who became matter for my sake'. This insight enables us not only to respond to the material creation, but to glorify God through our use of material things.

The celebration of creation in Catholic art, music and worship opens and enriches the scriptural texts about creation and in particular the first chapters of Genesis. The second creation account in Genesis implies that nature itself, through Adam, has a voice in saying what it is. Adam's vocation is to name the creatures.

A Responsive Creation

Every creature has potential to develop in response to the whole and contributes to the ecology of the whole by being what it is, a theme expressed poetically by Gerard Manley Hopkins in 'As kingfishers catch fire':

> Each mortal thing does one thing and the same;
> Deals out that being indoors each one dwells;

> Selves – goes itself; myself it speaks and spells
> Crying What I do is me: for that I came . . .

So this is a *responsive* creation, dreamed of by God and brought into being by God in such a way that it is open to development. It is both ordered and open. It is made by God and yet in some sense unfinished. This is how I see the encounter between Adam and the creatures in Genesis 2. Scripture tells us that the divine plan is not a fixed template so much as a living kit of parts. I think it is important to say this, because Scripture is being used to support a view of creation in the current controversy about human sexuality in a way which is not only profoundly unsympathetic to many of us but is, I believe, simply wrong. The difficulty comes in the interpretation of order. The Bible certainly implies that God orders creation according to his will. Torah is to be discerned in the ordering of the heavens as well as in the ordering of human life.

So what is order in creation? One way of looking at it is as a matter of limits and boundaries. In Genesis 1 order is a repeated repudiation of chaos, the *tohuwahbohu* 'waste and void' which is always threatening to break in. The order of creation is so fragile that it needs to be guarded. God creates by separation, division, the waters recede, the dry land appears, there is heaven and earth, darkness and light, sacred and profane, clean and unclean, God's people and not God's people. The guardian of this ordered creation in scriptural mythology is not God, but Satan, that servant of God who is described in the book of Job as a kind of heavenly policeman, prowling around looking for someone doing the wrong thing at the wrong time and in the wrong way. In such a universe *knowing your place* is the only appropriate response to God, and rewards and punishments are handed out according to whether you have behaved according to your station in the cosmic order. In practice knowing your place would mean understanding the hierarchy of being in a particular way. It would mean as a matter of course assuming that God has preferences. Usually this involves affirming the superiority of men to women. It need not, but can also involve justifying slavery and other kinds of social inequality, assuming that race is fixed and that certain races are superior to others.

Sexuality in a Responsive Creation

It is in this context that I think we should see our current problems about gender and sexuality, and it is these I now want to consider. Sex and gender are, of course, a part of creation, and sexuality has always been an area of both promise and pain within the Christian spiritual tradition. God invites all living things to reproduce after their kind, and makes the creatures, from birds and whales to humans with male and female characteristics. If you interpret biblical order exclusively in terms of boundaries in which each part of creation is required to behave in its divinely predetermined way, you may find all sorts of difficulties with what nature actually produces. Caterpillars become chrysalises and then become butterflies, changing their nature and properties through a life-cycle. Some creatures are hermaphrodites. When it comes to human beings there is, apparently, a God-given division of humanity into two genders, male and female. People *should* therefore be either male or female. But in nature a small but significant number of babies are born to whom it is difficult to assign either gender. Are these simply freaks, anomalies, who should not ever have been born? Are they tragedies, inviting the response that used to greet non-viable babies, 'the potter's hand has slipped'? Or is variation of this kind part of the way nature explores its own potential? Is it the way nature *responds*, in other words, to the mandate of creation, in ways that may be disastrous, but may also express latent potential?

What applies to gender could equally apply to sexual orientation. If orientation is merely a matter of boundaries then men *should* always be attracted to women and women to men. But, as we know, there are people whose sexual orientation is not to the opposite sex but to their own. There are also people who are not attracted to either gender, and people who, though attracted, choose not to express that in any particular relationship. These are all, on the first view of order, anomalous, though one of them, celibacy, has actually been regarded as an aid to sanctity. It is also a normative condition for priesthood in the Roman Catholic Church. This is because in the late-antique world in which Christianity emerged, the excitement and pleasure of sexual activity was extremely difficult to cope with. A trouble-free and sin-free life required what we would think of as extreme sexual repression.

People who think of sexual order in terms of boundaries find themselves having to deal with an inconsistency here. Celibacy is un-scriptural according to Genesis, but it is a positive help in the Lord's service according to Paul. To be celibate is to refuse the mandate of creation, and yet Jesus himself was celibate and childless. Conservative church teaching gets round this inconsistency by making celibacy a special vocation and by making being gay a kind of delusion. The choice to be celibate is taken as a virtue, but being gay is to be inherently disordered. Homosexual feeling can have nothing to do with the variations of creation because creation is fixed on this particular issue. The emphasis on the order of creation as being exclusively about boundaries has one appalling consequence, which is that it leads very easily to the view that suffering is a kind of punishment. Suffering is an outbreak of chaos, a return of the *tohuwabohu* – the fact that you suffer is a consequence of the fact that you have sinned. It is this assumption which lies behind the drama of the book of Job.

Job cries out to God for an answer to his miseries thinking that the answer will be a forensic one – either an acquittal or a condemnation. But what God produces is nothing like that at all. Instead of giving sentence for or against, he takes Job on a whirlwind tour of all the strange and fantastic phenomena of the universe, the stars and the sea, thunderbolts and rain, Behemoth and Leviathan, the snorting horse and the forgetful ostrich. What he reveals to Job is that there is indeed order, a profound order in creation, in which the strong and weak, the needy and the gifted, are bound together in mutual relationship. The creation is not an ascending hierarchy, nor is its order fixed beyond variation and response. It is, instead, a kind of communion.

So the Bible does not really understand creation in terms of a *fixed* order. It is rather more an order of development and reciprocity. The advantage of seeing the universe this way is that it resonates with our actual experience. This is a universe in which we are addressed, invited, wanted and required to act, and to which our primary responses are wonder and thanksgiving.

This is why Catholic Anglicans must stress, against the over prescriptive interpretations of creation around at the moment, that observation and reason are part of our theology of creation. They help us to get to grips with the whole of the scriptural message and not just with particular texts. So alongside Job we must put the psalms of creation which link creation to Torah, to that great gift of the law in which we are invited to delight. This is the divine law which marks the seasons and the times, for which boundaries are set not only for holding back chaos, but for the positive enriching of the world. Torah is both cosmological and ethical. It does not endorse the 'natural' order in which the rich grow richer and the poor become poorer. Torah delights in the raising of the poor and the restraining of the proud. It delights in variation and even novelty. What happens to us in this world is not a matter of rewards and punishments, but one where life comes from death and all are involved in the suffering and salvation of each.

Blessing for Variety

I love the spirit of thanksgiving for the gifts of creation expressed in the Jewish tradition of prayers of blessing. Consider this prayer of blessing on tasting any fruit for the first time in a season, or entering a new house, or wearing new clothes: 'Blessed art thou O Lord our God king of the universe who has kept us in life and preserved us, and has enabled us to reach this season.' But the same spirit also exists in a prayer to be said on seeing persons who are, from most people's point of view, deformed: 'Blessed art thou, O Lord our God king of the Universe who variest the form of thy creatures.'

In the universe of Job and the Psalms, perhaps also of Romans 8, there is a sketch of the kind of universe we know. A struggling, beautiful, evolving universe; a space-time manifold which is opaque to us in many ways, but also miraculously open to our observation and under-standing. This is a universe which can be interpreted in a christocentric way, in which suffering and glory, cross and resurrection, are held together in creative tension. As Mathew Fox put it in a television programme I was involved in during the 1990s:

> It is not just the light that is present in Christianity. It is also the woundedness, the wounds within the sacrificial offerings of the universe; the species that have gone extinct, the supernovae that died and exploded to give us the elements of our bodies.

Our current controversies invite us to ask, 'What does God mean by gay people?' It is a question we ought to be asking, though it is not easy for us as we do not yet appear to have been able to deal fully with the question, 'What does God mean by women?' Neither question can be answered ethically if the assumption is made from the outset that women or gay people are inferior and are of lesser worth in God's creation. In many parts of the world there is still a refusal of the right of women to exist as autonomous beings. In our world and in our church there is often a refusal to believe that gay people are made by God, even that gay people really exist at all. There are anecdotes in cir-culation of Christian male homosexuals, including ordi-nands and experienced priests, being told by their fathers in God that 'surely if they met the right woman' all would be well. It is from that point of virtual persecution that many of us now turn back to the Scriptures, to prayer and to the Eucharist.

The Sacrifice of Praise

I began by saying that a Catholic vision of creation takes us to the Eucharist, to thanksgiving. But it also takes us to suf-fering. Among those who have shared in the travail of cre-ation are the millions whose lives have been wrecked by religious bigotry and misplaced zeal, the cruelty both of religious ignorance and atheistic hatred of God. It is in the Eucharist that the themes of thanksgiving and suffering are brought together. The sacrifice of praise is also a memorial of the death of Christ. In the sacrifice of Christ is the ultimate breakdown of taboos. The veil of the temple is torn in two from the top to the bottom. This surely represents the exposure of human beings to the divine glory, and the divine penetration of human sinfulness. It speaks of the removal of harmful splits and separations from the human psyche, the making sacred of what was once profane, the healing of the unclean, and the renewing of creation. The end of all is thanksgiving. We behold the glory of God in the face of Jesus Christ, so that we may all see and become that glory which we behold.

2 The Glory of God Revealed in Natural Science

Fraser Watts

There is something strange about the idea of the glory of God being revealed in natural science. The very idea is paradoxical and invites a sceptical reaction. I cannot simply expound how the glory of God is revealed in natural science; it is necessary to address the inevitable scepticism about whether such a thing is possible.

There was a time when it would not have seemed as outlandish as it does now. If we go back to the seventeenth century, the century that culminated in John Ray's masterly book on *The Wisdom of God Manifested in the Works of Creation*, it would have been commonplace to see science as revealing the glory of God.

However, what we now call 'natural science' would have been called experimental method, or natural philosophy. It is part of the paradox that by the time 'natural science' had become a common term, the idea that it might reveal the glory of God was already becoming problematic. The explanation, of course, is that 'natural science' is an explicitly secular concept, a product of the Enlightenment. Scientific activity, by another name, can and has been deemed capable of revealing the glory of God. However, at the conceptual level, there is necessarily an uneasy relationship between 'science' and theology.

It is important to emphasise how enormously wide is the cultural gulf between the early modernity that came in with the seventeenth century (of which John Ray is an example), and the late modernity that succeeded it in the nineteenth century. Indeed, I have reached the conclusion that the differences between early and late modernity are so huge that it is thoroughly misleading to apply the same

term to both. It is a way of talking that leads us to exagge-
rate the similarities between the seventeenth and nineteenth centuries.

Early modernity was a profoundly religious age.
Religion may have taken new forms and new support for
religion may have been sought in experimental method
and philosophical argument. However, that should not
obscure how deeply religious a period the seventeenth century was, something which has been powerfully argued by
Amos Funkenstein in *Theology and the Scientific Imagination.*[1]
Even if one can find some of the seeds of later secularisa-
tion in the seventeenth century, it would be a gross historical misreading to see early modernity as in any sense a
secular period.

By late modernity the situation was very different, and
the changes were partly intellectual, partly social.[2]
Intellectually, a whole raft of secular concepts was being
introduced. The concept of science itself was one of them,
and the idea of the 'scientist' was even more a product of
late modernity.[3] The explicitly secular and materialistic concept of 'emotions' was replacing prior, more explicitly theological, concepts of passions and affections.[4] The concept of
human dignity was replacing prior, more explicitly theological, notions about human beings being created in the
image of God.

Also, society was beginning to fragment, and there was
a growing desire for areas of activity that would be free
from the influence of the church, and in that sense would be
'secular'. Churchgoing was still widespread in the late
nineteenth century but there was a growing sense of separation between religious and secular spheres of life. Science
was used by secularists such as Thomas Huxley as an
important tool in the drive for areas of cultural activity that
were free of church influence.

Another intriguing difference between early and late
modernity is how they regarded the sense of mystery and
wonder. Religious orthodoxy in the seventeenth century
was very suspicious of the sense of mystery and saw a
natural alliance between it and pantheism. It was part of
the purpose of natural theology to hold the line against
more pantheistic attitudes to nature, by subjecting nature to

detailed scrutiny and revealing its secrets.[5] In contrast, from late modernity onwards (and this is still very much true of our own time), we have instinctively come to see the sense of mystery and wonder as an ally of religion. The main enemy for religion to combat is no longer felt to be pantheism but materialistic reductionism, and a sense of mystery seems a natural ally of religion in that battle.

This raises the question of whether the idea of the glory of God being revealed in natural science is not a contradiction in terms. If science is an explicitly secular activity, how can it possibly reveal the glory of God? The fact that there has been such a radical divorce between theology and science over the last hundred years or so lends support to this. The majority of practising scientists today would be simply astonished at the idea that their research had anything to do with the glory of God.

However, it would be a mistake to conclude that science *cannot* reveal the glory of God. I submit that there is nothing inescapably secular about science. 'Science' may have been intended by some of its founding fathers to be an explicitly secular activity. However, that was never a monolithic view; there have always been those who have taken a more explicitly religious view of scientific activity. Also, it is perfectly possible for cultural movements such as science to change their colours. What we now know as science grew out of the natural philosophy and theology of the Enlightenment. It was the same movement, given a new twist. There is no reason at all why this movement should not take another twist back in a more theological direction.

The issues being raised here about natural science are very close to those raised by John Milbank in his *Theology and Social Theory*.[6] Milbank sees social theory as being a necessarily secular movement, one that is inherently opposed to theology, and which must be replaced by a theologically based approach to society. However, I believe he has made the mistake of paying too much attention to what particular founders of social science said. Firstly, they were not speaking for everyone in the social science movement. Also, we should pay attention to patterns of practice and activity, not just to what is said. Even if social science is surrounded by explicitly secular rhetoric, that does not make it impossible for it to be pursued with theological purposes. The same issues apply to natural science. Even if natural science was intended by some of its founding fathers to be secular, that does not mean that it necessarily has to be so.

Milbank's approach seems to imply that there can be a reconciliation of theology and science, whether social or natural, only if theology is in the driving seat, and science is made to rest on explicitly theological foundations and to serve theological purposes. It is, in some ways, a strange requirement in an intellectual climate that has come to be suspicious of foundationalism in all its forms. We have rightly come to be suspicious of the kind of natural theology that made science a foundation for theology. However, I would not want to switch to an opposing kind of foundationalism that tried to make theology a foundation for science. Neither do I see a reconciliation between theology and science as being dependent on theological foundationalism.

Should we then return to the outlook of the seventeenth century, to an approach to what we would now call 'science' that was closely intertwined with religious purposes, and which rested on theological foundations? Not necessarily. The way in which early modernity was able to see the glory of God revealed through the study of nature has come to have severe critics. There are both philosophical and theological problems with the natural theology of early modernity.

Philosophically, the arguments for God from natural philosophy simply did not work. More was being inferred theologically than could be justified, given the scientific premises. At very best, nature might be taken to suggest some kind of intelligent designer. It never lent strong support to belief in anything like the God of Christianity. David Hume's incisive critique of such arguments remains largely unanswerable.

Theologically, it is also doubtful whether the enterprise of natural theology was appropriate. There is perhaps something blasphemous about human beings treating God as an object of investigation, as though they could settle the question of whether or not he existed on the basis of scientific research. Observational method may have proved very useful in the natural philosophy of our early modernity, but it gave rise to a broader 'spectorial' consciousness, as Nicholas Lash has called it.[7] People imagined that they really could apply the same observational methods in establishing foundations for a theology as were proving fruitful in the study of nature. However, as Hegel said, 'God does not offer himself for observation', a dictum quoted by Lash in his trenchant critique of the assumptions of Enlightenment natural theology.[8]

Should we then abandon this attempt to serve theological purposes by the study of nature, and give up all hope of natural science revealing the glory of God? Not necessarily. I submit that there are ways in which a revived natural theology could proceed more satisfactorily than that of early modernity. However, it will need to be different philosophically and theologically, as well as being built on different scientific considerations.

It is no longer possible to conceive of natural theology as providing a foundation for revealed theology. That form of foundationalism, like most others, has to be abandoned. There is a place for a kind of natural theology but it needs to proceed in parallel with revealed theology and in dialogue with it. It is not capable of doing all that is required to provide a foundation for revealed theology. Revealed theology is not going to find secure foundations anywhere, whether in revelation, religious experience, or anything else. The processes of interpretation, which are a necessary part of any conceivable foundation for revealed theology, undercut any claim that its foundations are secure.

Philosophically, also, much revision is needed to the natural theology of early modernity. Natural theology has often been presented as a set of arguments for the existence of God, and the natural theology of early modernity grew, in some ways, out of the arguments of Aquinas' 'five ways'. However, it may be a mistake to see science as providing any kind of *argument* for the existence of God. The notion of argument implies a sharper separation between premises and conclusions than is appropriate here; it suggests that theological conclusions can be reached on the basis of scientific premises. I doubt whether that is possible.

The issue here is rather like the one that arises when people try to reach moral conclusions on the basis of factual premises, an enterprise that has been labelled the 'naturalistic fallacy'. However, interestingly, philosophers now often take a less dismissive attitude to ethical arguments that draw on factual considerations than used to be the case. The moderate consensus would now be that, even though factual considerations cannot justify ethical conclusions in and of themselves, nevertheless they are relevant to ethical arguments. Factual considerations are neither sufficient for ethical conclusions, nor are they irrelevant to them.

The very notion of a 'fact' is, of course, itself open to criticism. There is no factual neutrality. As Thomas Nagel has put it, there is no 'view from nowhere' that permits the neutral observation of facts.[9] There is no moral neutrality from which factual observations can be introduced into ethical arguments. Similarly, there is no theoretical neutrality from which they can be introduced into scientific arguments. As Hanson has memorably remarked, 'all data are theory laden'.[10]

This leads to a view of natural theology in which there is a less clear separation between science and theology than is often assumed. Rather than a to and fro between two very distinct domains that are unbridgeably different, we need to think of a much closer intertwining, indeed an integration between them. As Owen Barfield, friend of C. S. Lewis has remarked 'the ball is tossed to and fro from the theory to experiment from experiment back again to theory'. However, only a full realisation of the intimate relationship between language, theory and experiment will enable us to 'escape from the prison of our fragmented language and a fragmented science – and ultimately from the fragmented civilisation they have produced'.[11]

It is interesting in this connection to recall that the word 'theory' has its origins in the Greek 'theoria', which is more a matter of vision than the set of propositions that we now associate with a 'theory'. This piece of etymology provided the title for a journal published by the Epiphany

Philosophers from 1966 to 1981. It was called the *Theoria to Theory*. It was intended to point towards a kind of science that would be closer to contemplation, and which would sit more easily alongside contemplative religion.

What I am suggesting we need is a natural theology that is more a *contemplation* of nature than a philosophical argument from premises about nature. That is something that Del Ratzsch of Calvin College has suggested in his book, *Nature, Design, and Science.*[12] In developing this position, he has taken his cue from the Scottish, common-sense philosopher, Thomas Reid, who talks about how we can simply find ourselves in the grip of a conviction on the basis of sense data, without that conviction following logically from the sense data. According to Ratzsch, the features of design that are often taken to be the premise of natural theology arguments are more a matter of what we recognise in nature.

This brings natural theology closer to the form that it takes in the Hebrew Bible. There, in the Psalms and other wisdom literature, we find a good deal of reflection on nature as being imbued with the glory of God. The classic text is the first verse of Psalm 19, 'The heavens declare the glory of God, and the firmament showeth of his handywork.' James Barr, in a helpful commentary on biblical natural theology, and in a fashion that is similar to Del Ratzsch, suggests that this is more a matter of how nature is perceived than of what can be inferred from nature.[13]

Seeing that glory of God in the natural world thus becomes an occasion for what Ian Ramsey used to call a 'disclosure' or 'ah-ha' experience. The role of faith here is more that of presupposition than conclusion. It joins with what we can see in nature to produce a faith-imbued disclosure of the glory of God. We can perhaps apply here some words about the role of faith from Thomas Aquinas' well-known eucharistic hymn: 'Faith alone the true heart waketh to behold the mystery' and 'Faith, our outward sense befriending, makes the inward vision clear'.

What aspects of the natural world can lead to this sense of the glory of God being disclosed? As has already been noted, there is the classical 'design' argument, that the world gives the appearance of having been well designed.

However, there has been an increasing shift towards 'eutax-iological' considerations, based on the lawfulness, regularity and intelligibility of the world.

There are also considerations about the fruitfulness of the universe. The universe seems to have characteristics that lead it to be fruitful, in the sense of being suitable for the development of carbon-based life, and eventually for the development of human beings. Theologically, that leads to reflection, not just on the glory of God, but on his purposes. It is not difficult to see it as consistent with the purposes of God that he should create a universe that would give rise to creatures capable of receiving his revelation.

So what is the role of natural science in contributing to a vision of the natural world as being imbued with the glory of God, or reflecting his purposes? One important consideration is whether the sense of the glory of God is enhanced in any way by the apparent inexplicability of the world. Here, intuitions have been quite diverse. The well-known version of the design argument put forward by Thomas Paley at the beginning of the nineteenth century traded upon the assumption that the world as we observe it would be inexplicable without postulating a designer. For him, if you find a watch on the heath, there is no plausible alternative but to postulate a watch-maker. Seeing God in the natural world has thus often tended to be an argument from ignorance, and to trade on a sense of mystery.

This kind of argument is inclined to run into the sand. For Paley, there was no other explanation of why species were so well designed for their habitats, other than that a divine designer had created them to be so. When natural selection provided an alternative explanation, the design argument, as Paley had propounded it, collapsed. However, this need not necessarily happen.

Here, the contrast between the appearance of design in the world, and its orderliness and intelligibility, is relevant. Considerations of design are vulnerable to being undermined by scientific advances. However, that is not also true of considerations of the orderliness and intelligibility of the world. On the contrary, the more science proceeds, the more it establishes the orderliness and intelligibility of the world. Thus, in as far as its orderliness leads to a sense of the world being imbued with the glory of God, science increasingly supports such a sense. The important point here, and one that Richard Swinburne has emphasised very clearly, is that theology is not explaining what is scientifically inexplicable. On the contrary, it is explaining *why* the universe is scientifically explicable.[14]

There is an interesting two-way connection here. The fact that science has flourished more in Christian culture than anywhere else can be attributed, in part, to the fact that Christianity assumes the lawfulness of the world. Further, it assumes that this lawfulness is contingent and therefore something that needs to be understood by empirical investigation. Thus, Christian presuppositions about the orderliness of the universe seem to have given rise to science and the confirmation of that orderliness that emerges from science further strengthens Christian assumptions.

There are two broad areas of science that have contributed to the sense of the world being created by God and reflecting his glory, cosmology and biology. Which has been used most by natural theology has depended, to some extent, on cultural background. In the classic heyday of natural theology, cosmological consideration seemed to have been more important on the continent, while biological considerations were more important in Britain. Today, biological arguments are regarded with much suspicion in America, where creationism is more of a bogey, but get a better hearing in Britain. We will begin with cosmology.

There is no doubt that the universe is remarkably fine-tuned for carbon-based life. Francis Crick, no friend of religion, once remarked that it looks as though someone has 'monkeyed' with the physics. In order to get the stable matter on which life can develop, it is necessary for the force of expansion coming from the Big Bang, and the force of gravity counteracting it, to be very finely balanced. This is indeed the case. In fact, the balance is so fine that it is hard to judge which will eventually win out, whether the universe will continue to expand indefinitely, or whether at some point the force of gravity will win out and the universe will end in a 'big crunch'. It is not important for our present argument which will eventually be the case.

However, the balance between expansion and contraction seems exactly right for the universe to be fruitful.

The universe is also remarkably fine-tuned for the production of carbon, which is the basis of life. Carbon is not an easy element to produce, as it requires the collision of three helium nuclei. That would be highly unlikely by chance, but there is a nuclear resonance that is exactly right to facilitate the production of carbon. Once formed in stars, carbon needs to be dispersed. Neutrinos play a key role in that but the strength of the weak nuclear force has to be exactly right. If it was weaker, neutrinos would flood out on their own without pushing carbon or other elements out. If it were stronger, the neutrinos would get involved in reactions in the core of the star, and not escape at all. More generally, the balance between the four basic forces (gravity, electromagnetism, the strong nuclear force which holds atomic nuclei together, and the weak nuclear force responsible for radioactive decay) have to be pretty much exactly as they are for life to develop.

These considerations about the fine-tuning of the universe are sometimes referred to as the 'anthropic' principle. I think that is an unhelpful way of describing them. They are concerned with considerations that make the universe fine-tuned for carbon-based life. They are nothing to do with human life. An entirely different set of considerations comes into the question of how likely carbon-based life is to result in a human-like species.

So far, we have no scientific explanation of why the universe should be so finely tuned. However, the question arises of whether we are in a situation rather like that of Paley, who had no idea that 50 years later Darwin would undercut his argument from design with a theory of evolution by natural selection. Though this is very much not my area of science, it seems to me not out of the question that we might arrive at an understanding of the universe as a homeostatic system that gave rise to a fruitful balance between expansion and contraction. Might we also arrive at a scientific understanding of why the basic forces of the universe are balanced in the way they are?

There are some who would argue that we are dealing here with such foundational matters that they are in principle beyond the scope of what science could ever explain. My instinct is to be cautious about such a position. However, what I want to emphasise is that theological reflection on the fine-tuning of the universe does not depend on a continuing lack of scientific explanation. On the contrary, the more we understand about how and why the universe is remarkably fine-tuned, the more those who have the eyes of faith may be inclined to perceive the glory of God, and his purposes, as reflected in that fine-tuning.

At present, little headway is being made with such possible scientific explanations. However, there is much interest in the possibility of multiple universes. The argument is that, with an infinite, or at least very large, series of universes you are bound to get a highly fruitful one by chance somewhere within the series. It is a possibility that is difficult to argue against. However, the postulation of such a series of universes seems profligate and unattractive. Also, it depends on the relevant factors that contribute to fine-tuning being randomly distributed across the vast series of universes, and that may not turn out to be the right assumption.

Let me now turn from cosmology to biology. It is best to concede at the outset that there are currently no biological arguments for the existence of God that are remotely compelling. However, I am not daunted by that because, as I have already indicated, I do not think that natural theology should primarily take the form of arguments. It is more a matter of seeing the world through the eyes of faith but in a way that is informed by scientific study. That kind of more contemplative natural theology is perfectly viable in the biological arena.

We find it, for example, in Charles Raven, theologian and naturalist: 'Here is beauty – whatever the philosophers and art critics who have never looked at a moth may say – beauty that rejoices and humbles, beauty remote from all that is meant by words like random or purposeless, utilitarian or materialistic, beauty in its impact and affects akin to the authentic encounter with God.'[15]

However, it is on evolutionary biology that I particularly want to focus. Let me make clear that I have no particular sympathy with those who argue against natural selection as a mechanism of evolution. Like the early Christian Darwinists, such as Charles Kingsley, I assume that evolution is God's way of creating species. There is probably much more to evolution than we have yet understood, and I guess that our eventual scientific theory of evolution will include other ingredients apart from raw natural selection. However, I do not want to join those, such as Behe, who have argued that there are cases of irreducible complexity, like the eye, that could not have come about through natural selection at all.

Though it is no doubt possible to develop a biological natural theology that claims that the natural world has a designed quality, or one that trades on the intelligibility of the natural world, the most compelling form of biological natural theology focuses on its fruitfulness. The most striking fact about evolution is the way primitive microorganisms have eventually developed into an intelligent form of life such as *homo sapiens*. Nevertheless, the notion of 'direction' in evolution has been controversial and people have been wary of assuming that human beings are the pinnacle of evolution. However, it seems to me undeniable that there has been direction in the evolution, towards creatures of increasing complexity, and especially creatures of greater information processing capacity.

If we concede directionality in evolution, it invites a theological commentary in terms of it being the purpose of God that intelligent life should eventually emerge out of the original, primitive micro-organisms. However, for that theological interpretation of directionality to be justifiable, it is necessary to assume some kind of inevitability about what eventually emerged, that it was not just a random accident. There is a vigorous scientific debate about how far evolution is a purely chance process, as Stephen Jay Gould amongst others has maintained,[16] or how far there is an inevitability about the evolution of creatures like human beings. Simon Conway Morris has emerged as an effective champion of the latter position.[17] His argument is built around the phenomenon of convergence in evolution, that there are certain forms of life that evolve quite independently in different contexts. In his view, that supports the conclusion that there is an inevitability about their emergence.

It is important here to be careful not to suggest that evolution had to take exactly the path it did, or that the intelligent, relational beings it has produced had to be exactly like human beings. However, I do believe it is plausible to argue that there was such evolutionary advantage in information processing that it was inevitable that creatures with an advanced capacity for it would emerge sooner or later, and that when they did they would have a massive advantage in natural selection terms. That superior capacity for information processing seems to be what has underpinned the human capacity for reflective self-consciousness and relationality, including the capacity to receive God's revelation of himself and to grow into relationship to him. Thus, evolution seems to be designed to achieve God's purpose in creation.

I have argued here for a version of natural theology that is contemplative rather than a matter of philosophical argument, that is informed by scientific inquiry without trying to use science to justify religious conclusions, and which is enhanced by the further development of science rather than depending on its continuing lacunae. It is a form of natural theology in which faith and natural science come together to enhance our wonder at the glory of God revealed in creation.

So, can we recover the consciousness of the author of Psalm 19 that 'the heavens declare the glory of God'? Not quite. That, I believe, reflected an old animistic consciousness that has faded for ever. We no longer have the same kind of instinctive sense of spirit inhabiting nature. However, I believe it is possible to build a new kind of animism. It will be freely chosen, deliberate, and knowing, rather than effortless and instinctive as the old animism was. Because it is knowing, it can be informed by natural science in a way that the old animism did not need to be. Because it is deliberate, it will need to be the fruit of spiritual practice and discipline in a way that used not to be necessary.

It will involve a changed relationship between nature and spirit. In the old animism, the spirit was felt to be speaking to us through nature. The new animism can be seen as an eventual fulfilment of Christ's promise of the Spirit to 'dwell within us', as St John's Gospel puts it. That gift of the Spirit opens up the possibility of a spirit-imbued perception of nature. The direction has changed, no longer the spirit speaking to us from nature, but the Spirit within us influencing our perception of nature and enabling us to see the glory of God there.

Humanity needs to learn to make better use of the gift of the Spirit to perceive glory in this way. I do believe this is possible. Indeed, I believe it was one of the central purposes of Christ's gift of the Spirit to humanity to make possible this new, spirit-imbued perception of the glory of God in creation. Humanity is called to turn that possibility into an actuality. Given the way in which our natural environment is currently under threat, it is urgent that we should do so.

Notes

1 Amos Funkenstein, *Theology and the Scientific Imagination: from the Middle Ages to the Seventeenth Century* (Princeton: Princeton University Press, 1986).

2 John Hedley Brooke, *Science and Religion: Some Historical Perspectives* (Cambridge: Cambridge University Press, 1991).

3 Stephen Toulmin, *Cosmopolis: The Hidden Agenda of Modernity* (New York: Free Press, 1990).

4 Thomas Dixon, 'The Psychology of the Emotions in Britain and America in the Nineteenth Century: The Role of Religious and Antireligious Commitments' in *Osiris* 16 (2001), pp. 288–320.

5 Mary Midgley, *Science as Salvation: A Modern Myth and its Meaning* (London: Routledge, 1992).

6 John Milbank, *Theology and Social Theory: Beyond Secular Reason* (Oxford: Blackwell, 1990).

7 Nicholas Lash, 'Observation, Revelation and the Posterity of Noah' in *The Beginning and the End of Religion* (Cambridge: Cambridge University Press), pp. 75–92.

8 ibid., p. 80.

9 Thomas Nagel, *The View from Nowhere* (New York: Oxford University Press, 1986).

10 N. R. Hanson, *Patterns of Discovery* (Cambridge: Cambridge University Press, 1958).

11 Owen Barfield, *The Rediscovery of Meaning, and Other Essays* (Middletown, CT: Wesleyan University Press, 1977), p. 138.

12 Delvin Lee Ratzsch, *Nature, Design, and Science: The Status of Design in*

Natural Science (Albany: State University of New York Press, 2001).

13 James Barr, *Biblical Faith and Natural Theology: The Gifford Lectures for 1991*, delivered in the University of Edinburgh (Oxford: Clarendon Press, 1993).

14 Richard Swinburne, *Is There a God?* (Oxford: Oxford University Press, 1996).

15 Charles Raven, *Natural Religion and Christian Theology* (Cambridge: Cambridge University Press, 1953).

16 Stephen Jay Gould, *Wonderful Life: The Burgess Shale and the Nature of History* (London: Hutchinson Radius, 1990).

17 Simon Conway Morris, *The Crucible of Creation: The Burgess Shale and the Rise of Animals* (Oxford: Oxford University Press, 1998).

3 The Glory of God Revealed in Art and Music: Learning from Pagans

David Brown

It is often the seeming accidentals of human life that have the most decisive impact upon what we do and say, and in that particular respect this essay is no different. I sat down to write it at the same time as I was due to preach a sermon on what is often regarded as one of the most problematic texts in the New Testament, Jesus' encounter with the Syrophoenician woman. The reader will no doubt recall the incident.[1] Jesus had ventured into the Gentile territory around the ancient seaports of Tyre and Sidon, home to one branch of the Phoenician race, the other now sadly depleted as a result of Rome's laying waste its major city at Carthage in modern Tunisia. A request to heal the woman's daughter is met with the comment from Jesus that 'it is not right to take the children's bread and throw it to the dogs', to which the woman responds: 'Yes, Lord; yet even the dogs under the table eat the children's crumbs.' Commentators often try to lessen the severity of Jesus' words by describing them as ironic or even, since a diminutive is used, as affectionate: his talk is then really of 'little doggies'.[2] I for one just don't believe it. The longer version in Matthew emphasises how Jesus saw his role as being essentially to 'the lost sheep of Israel'. So the woman's reaction to his use of this common dismissive way of speaking about the Phoenicians must surely have brought Jesus up with a start, and made him think anew about the importance of the Gentiles in God's economy of salvation, kept as they were to a firmly subservient role in the Old Testament view of the last times.[3] Perhaps it is even the case that it is thanks to this exchange that Jesus came up eventually with the parable of the Good Samaritan, with the key role now assigned to someone of the mixed race that the Jews so despised. We shall of course never know for certain, but if the incident did play a crucial role in shaping Jesus' consciousness, such an explanation would provide a reason why the story was preserved despite its potential embarrassment for the later, largely Gentile church.

Many Christians object to such a way of thinking about Jesus, making him partly dependent as it does for his developing consciousness on the insights of others. But is not that precisely what the glory of the incarnation is all about, a real entering into our humanity and so learning and growing in understanding in very similar ways to ourselves? Austin Farrer reminds us of how much Jesus must have owed to someone totally unknown to us, the local village rabbi at Nazareth, but of course there would have been many others. Rowan Williams puts it succinctly: Jesus 'learned how to be human' and that meant learning within a specific context, including of course the parental home, and so from Mary and Joseph.[4]

All this may seem far from our theme, but it is not. Just as the temptation to see Jesus as a totally self-contained individual must be resisted if the incarnation is to be treated seriously, so, I believe, must a similar temptation about revelation in general. Readers familiar with my more recent academic writings will know that I have argued this point at considerable length, particularly as this applies to the notion of developing tradition, which is what I take revelation to be.[5] Triggers can come from outside as much as from within, in encouraging new ways of thinking about God, and so providing a deeper understanding of his will and purposes for humanity. This is not the place to pursue such arguments. Instead, I want to effect a much more limited aim. A constant temptation among Christians when looking at art or music is to view their role, when legitimate, as at most illustrative, confirming or deepening faith but never challenging or subverting it. It is therefore hardly surprising that there is so much bad Christian art and music around, if even the more informed among us want to keep their influence in a safe pair of Christian hands, such as Rembrandt or Rouault in art, Bach or Bruckner in music. The more liberal minded, in spreading the net more widely, may believe themselves immune from such criticism, but often the same fault is still there: art seen as merely illustrative of what is already believed on other grounds. I shall use an Oxford academic to highlight the latter problem, and towards the end of this essay a Cambridge theologian to illustrate how the fault affects a more conservative mind. But in the main I want through the use of specific examples to encourage readers to reflect for themselves. Jesus, if I am right, learnt from a pagan; might not we also?

These days 'pagan' has become almost a pejorative term, equivalent to 'atheist'. That is not how I shall use the word. The Syrophoenician woman is herself likely to have been a worshipper of the local god, Eshmun. What I have in mind, therefore, is those who appear beyond the bounds of Christian orthodoxy but still engaged with the question of God. An interesting musical example that also raises the question of inspiration as such comes from the work of the German composer Hans Pfitzner (d. 1949). Nominally a Protestant, he seems to have moved in and out of faith.[6] There is insufficient documentation to inform us whether or not his opera *Palestrina* of 1917 was written in one mood or its opposite. The theme, however, is clear. In the sixteenth century Palestrina saved polyphony for the Church despite considerable opposition from the Council of Trent, worried as it was by the fact that counterpoint in later medieval music no longer allowed the words of the mass to be clearly audible. The legend was that Palestrina's *Missa Papae Marcelli* did the trick. This is unlikely if only because the pope to whom it was dedicated was dead within three weeks of taking office and Palestrina himself was forced to leave his job at the Sistine Chapel because he was married. But what concerns us here is how Pfitzner exploits that theme.

The decisive moment of inspiration comes at the end of the first act, when Palestrina first hears past composers urging him on, then angelic voices and the muse of his late wife.[7] That brief outline is probably sufficient to indicate that Pfitzner was struggling between two competing conceptions, that the source of the inspiration lay in God (the angels) or more simply in loyalty to his vocation as a composer (the more human voices). But does it matter in terms of either Palestrina or Pfitzner having something to say to us? We now know how incredibly complex a process of transmission lies behind the words of Scripture, and how hard it would be to claim one moment in that process as decisive. This is not to argue against divine inspiration, but it is to protest against focusing too narrowly as though only what lays claim to inspiration must be seen as part of God's providential guidance. Rather, what matters is the capacity, however this originates, of certain words or non-verbal forms to speak to us, and thus lead us into new ways of understanding our tradition as we attempt to absorb these new triggers to thought.

So Pfitzner's own views are less important than the challenge they embody: is verbal comprehension always an essential part of worship or not? At the decisive moment Pfitzner introduces a female angel singing in A major the opening line of Palestrina's original *Kyrie*, to which Pfitzner's composer responds by himself changing key to echo Palestrina's own warm tones, thus abandoning his own earlier gloom (in C sharp minor). That mood of interchange is then carried right throughout the scene with the Latin of the mass clearly audible against the German of the composer. It is a wonderfully lyrical and Romantic piece of writing, but the irony is that most of us now hearing the work in German and Latin might well conclude that the music is enough on its own, even if we don't fully understand the words. So in this work we can appreciate Pfitzner's discussion of the dilemma, whether or not he was a Christian at the time, and also even draw a different conclusion from the main theme round which the opera is built – that words need not always be audible for a religious dimension to be appropriated.

Words, however, did play a key part in the story of the annunciation. I have already criticised elsewhere Oxford's John Drury's treatment of several paintings of the annunciation in London's National Gallery.[8] He reads them as illustrative of universal human themes that we can all easily accept rather than paying attention to the more challenging themes of historical context, and so to arguments such as about who should kneel to whom, and why Mary is presented in all three as reading. The former raises major theological issues but it is the latter on which I wish to focus here because it takes us beyond theology in the narrower sense and into wider issues of cultural dependence. Put Western and Eastern images of the annunciation alongside one another and immediately some major contrasts are to be observed. Orthodox icons continue to this day to portray Mary at work spinning as she hears the angel's call. That was once also the Western image but the typical later medieval and post-medieval form is quite different. Here Mary is reading. This may seem a matter of no great moment. Certainly, in terms of the origins of the image not much was at stake, for texts first appear with the words of the angel on an accompanying banderol and so book or banderol was simply a way of making the appropriate allusion. But eventually the book appears on its own without accompanying justification and that, I believe, is of considerable significance, for any remaining pretence of an historical record has now been abandoned. The Virgin Mary was almost certainly illiterate and so the Orthodox convention is nearer to Mary's actual practice. Yet as representation it seems to me mere illustration and so rather dull, whereas in the West in the later Middle Ages artists are in effect engaging in discussion of what contemporary women might legitimately do. Client and artist (whether devout or not) were arguing for women's access to literacy, initially through prayer books such as the newly popular Books of Hours, but also in due course more widely. So we must not think that arguments over women's rights only began in modern times. Paintings of the Christian story, whether by devout artists or otherwise, were challenging Christians to think anew.

But there is no reason to remain in the distant past in our search for pertinent examples. The twentieth century is often described as a time of loss of faith and in many ways that is true, but a surprising number of artists continued to engage actively with the Christian faith in their art. The natural tendency of Christians has been to focus on those who are explicit believers such as Norman Adams or Mark Cazalet, James MacMillan or John Tavener, but to do so exclusively would be merely to repeat the mistake against which I have been protesting. God does not just speak through the like-minded. So let me now take two pagan artists who challenge our understanding of the Christian faith in ways that lead, I believe, to its deepening and not to its destruction.

My first example comes from Jesus' childhood, Max Ernst's *The Infant Jesus chastised by the Virgin Mary* (1926).[9] Where this painting challenges us is over the question of how full an incarnation we are actually prepared to believe in. For if Jesus completely entered into what it was to be an ordinary human being, growing up in one particular set of circumstances rather than another, would he not have been subject to the normal conventions of that culture, and so corporal punishment have been part of his life experience just as it would have been for every other boy in the ancient world? Such a conclusion is often resisted on the supposition that, had Jesus merited punishment, he could not possibly have been morally perfect. But this is to import into childhood judgements that are really only fully applicable to adult behaviour. Child psychologists inform us that children like to test the limits of their parents' tolerance not just as a way of irritating them but rather in order to discover boundaries in relation to which they will feel secure and self-contained. Jesus as a child would surely have been no different. So it is not so much that he sinned as that, like the rest of us, such testing of the boundaries was his way of discovering set limits, guides to what is right and what is wrong.

Rather more, though, is at stake than what my remarks hitherto might seem to imply. For despite the flippancy of elements in this painting such as the lost halo on the ground or the three Surrealist witnesses in the background, Ernst is also telling us something about his own loss of faith. His artist father had once employed him as a model to represent a young Jesus who was angelically perfect. No, indicates the adult Ernst, now no longer a believer: that is not the sort of saccharine God in whom I could ever believe. Not that this point had never been made before. A medieval roof boss in Nuremberg of the five-year-old Jesus being dragged to school or Simone Martini's depiction of the twelve-year-old sulking at his parents' reprimand might have been used to make the same observation. It is a lesson that as yet has still not been fully absorbed by Christianity. The agnostic Ernst thus constitutes a continuing challenge to any notion of the infant Jesus as 'our childhood's pattern', 'mild' and 'obedient'.[10] Even Luke himself seems not immune from such criticism.

Consider now how a convinced atheist might help. That is how Francis Bacon understood himself, and yet he was obsessed with the crucifixion, which appears in one form or another in so many of his paintings. Indeed, on his postwar relaunch he decided to destroy everything prior to his famous *Three Studies for Figures at the Base of a Crucifixion* of 1944. The agony he presents is usually so unqualifiedly awful that his message is scarcely in doubt, that there cannot conceivably be any answer to the problem of suffering. If 'answer' is hardly the right word, Christians can scarcely countenance quite so negative a verdict. After all, John's Gospel repeatedly informs us that God's glory was to be seen even in so terrible an act as the crucifixion.[11] Yet even Bacon seems to yield at one point in a way that is both illuminating and challenging.

His erstwhile lover, George Dyer, committed suicide in a Paris hotel room in 1973 and Bacon portrayed the scene in one of his triptychs.[12] While the side panels depict Dyer first being sick into a basin and then dying on the toilet seat, the central image is of him as he enters the room, casting a shadow like a great bird of prey. It is what hangs above, though, that is of particular interest. It is a naked light bulb, suspended in a V shape from the exposed cord. Neither the hotel nor its clients were that impoverished, and so it seems to me correct to infer that for once Bacon is overcome by his love for Dyer to say something which did not come naturally to his cynical and promiscuous nature.[13] Obsessed at times by sado-masochistic desires, he also liked verbally humiliating, before his educated friends, the working class boys whom he picked up. Yet, borrowing partly from Grünewald's Isenheim Altarpiece (for the angle of the cord) and partly from Picasso (for the light bulb) here he is declaring that his love will live on, and indeed he continued to paint Dyer even after his death. The naked light bulb and the angle of the cord thus alike hint at continuity, at hope, at love.

None of this can of course possibly turn Bacon into a Christian. The challenge is rather more subtle than that. These days when Christians want to support gay relationships they often seek to model them as closely as possibly on heterosexual ones and so talk of the need for exclusive commitments. This is not the place to enter into the rights and wrongs of such questions. All I want to do is alert the reader to the way in which Bacon struggling to express love draws our attention to its presence even in highly flawed or promiscuous relationships. We all like to draw simple boundaries but life is not quite like that. So even if the church does change its rules, it will still not have answered all the questions of how it is to support those who struggle in imperfection to discover something of the reflection of divine love in their relationships with their fellow human beings.

In the case of Schubert's last song cycle *Winterreise*, it is not the death of another that is being faced, but his own death. Schubert's early mass settings are so enjoyable and uplifting that we are often inclined to forget his unorthodoxy, his reluctance, for example, to include belief in the Church in his settings of the creed. Now here he is facing death from syphilis, as he sets to music a cycle of poems written by the contemporary Prussian poet, Wilhelm Müller (d. 1827). Their nominal theme is an individual taking a walk, as he seeks to come to terms with rejection in love. Schubert, however, deepens their meaning and makes the issue much more than just the typical Romantic exaggerated despair and longing for death. After quite a number of tempestuous and troubled songs, with the last three there seems a real attempt to face impending death. A song about courage in the absence of the gods leads into a mysterious vision of three suns,[14] with the final song then a meditation on a lonely hurdy-gurdy player working on the edge of town. Not once is there any reference whatsoever to the Christian God nor to heaven, and yet, despite some who wish to speak of atheism, there is rather more than just the mere acceptance of the inevitable. It is more like an achieved, if somewhat bleak, serenity in the face of suffering and death. Of course, much will depend on performance and interpretation. In later life Dietrich Fischer-Dieskau, for example, takes the last song more slowly than he did earlier in his career and so succeeds in stressing that acceptance.[15] Again, Ian Bostridge speaks of a 'religious aura' particularly in respect of the suns' song.[16] That would seem confirmed by the fact that Schubert was writing his last mass about the same time, and it has a mystery and solemnity about it that the earlier ones lack.[17]

This is not to say that *Winterreise* is really Christianity in disguise. It is not. Where, though, it does address Christianity, it seems to me, is in our often too glib appeals to resurrection and life after death. Schubert seems to me to be saying that even where life is bleak and one feels thrown onto the edge of things like the hurdy-gurdy player, acceptance of one's destiny is important, perseverance is vital whatever the future may bring. To look only to the marvellous coda to our lives in closer intimacy with God is to forget that this life too has had its value and its integrity, even if there is nothing beyond, and for that we should be accepting, even grateful.

Drury would wish to see landscape painting as marking a similar narrowing of focus onto this world. He declares that such works 'exemplify the . . . movement of Christian painting into the secular . . . [L]ike the sacred bread in the Eucharist . . . the myth has been consumed into the real, the other into the familiar.'[18] What one misses from his account is the way in which such art often continues to try to engage with God's interaction with the world at a deep level and so substantial, if now more implicit, theological claims are still made. Take, for instance, as apparently conventional a painter as Constable. Prints of his works adorn many a modern household wall, but few seem aware that he was a devout high churchman, many of whose canvases are a medium for reflection on divine presence in the world. Everyone knows and loves the familiar images of Salisbury Cathedral. I'm sure the present Bishop of Salisbury would never be as naïve as one of his predecessors (John Fisher) and object, as he did, to the presence of clouds in one of these, simply because they seemed to give too pessimistic a view of the church.[19] We laugh, but

51

unfortunately our level of reading of art, our desire simply for confirmation of what we already believe as Christians, can sometimes be just as bad. It may appear initially that Constable himself fell into precisely that fault in one of his later versions where the building is set against a rainbow emerging after a storm.[20] Certainly Constable wanted to allude to the way in which the established church seemed once again secure after all the threats made against it in the run-up to the great Reform Bill of 1832. But there is more than just symbolism here, a sort of one-to-one correspondence between church and nature with a piece of natural imagery only borrowed to speak of God's real sphere of action in the church. What is going on is much more a question of parallelism, of us being invited to view the providential hand of God already operating in one sphere (nature) as confirmation of divine action in the other (the church). In other words, Constable is actively challenging his fellow Christians of the time to think of God in a more immanent and involved way. If that was in some ways easier for him because in his day the biblical story of the origin of the rainbow was still being taken literally, the basic challenge is still there for us to think of Christ's church as still subject to such care, even when it appears to be going in a direction that we don't particularly like.

If that observation dissatisfies, later in the century, we may note, landscape art was to be used to issue a radical challenge: that Christianity was not immanentist enough. Vincent van Gogh had spent some of his youth as a missionary in the Belgian coalmines. Although he eventually lost his Christian faith, some of his late paintings leave us in no doubt that he was still wrestling with what might constitute a satisfactory account of God's relation to the world. Christianity he sees as too particularist and too transcendent. That is the implicit message behind his image of *The Sower*, where the sun forms a halo around the man as he works, or still more dramatically in his copying of Rembrandt's *Raising of Lazarus* where this time the sun is actually made to replace Christ, the universal healer instead of what he has come to see as too narrowing and too constrictive a Christ.[21] As Christians we are bound to think van Gogh wrong in this estimate, but that does not mean that we should not listen and heed the warning in the dangers of too transcendent a God, a Christianity that despite the incarnation removes God too far from this world and ordinary people's lives; or of too particularist a Christ that neglects the world as a whole.

It was an issue with which another landscape artist from about the same time also wrestled. Van Gogh committed suicide in 1890 and Cézanne returned to the practice of the Catholic faith the following year. Throughout the last years of his life he used a local mountain, Mont Sainte-Victoire, to work through what the relation between God and the world might be. In a few canvases the stress is very much on transcendence, with a sharp line drawn between the mountain and the surrounding terrain, but for the most part the colours and contours of the two interact and so evoke a lively sense of a God at one and the same time transcendent and immanent.[22] My point is a simple one. Theology can be done through landscape art. The artist is not necessarily simply reflecting nature, he can also be asking questions pertinent to theology, and for that to be so it is by no means essential that the artist must be a practising Christian. Van Gogh had lost his Christian faith and Cézanne was clearly still struggling with his.

My general theme is, I hope by now clear: art can of course illustrate faith but to insist that this is its only appropriate role is to belittle its achievements. Whether there are specific allusions to Christianity or not, it can offer a religious vision that we need to take seriously and engage with. As one last example of the problem let me take a conservative Cambridge theologian. David Ford has some excellent things to say in his book *Self and Salvation*. Yet, although there are also quite a number of artistic, poetic and musical allusions, none seems ever to rise above the level of the purely illustrative. It is almost as though the author already knows what he wants to say and then looks round for confirmatory examples. The result is the very strange irony with which the book ends.[23] Ford quotes one of the poems of his friend, Michael O'Siadhail who uses jazz to illustrate his view of heaven. Ford's final words then take up the title of a jazz piece to which O'Siadhail had already alluded, *A Love Supreme*. Ford seems to take the quotation as endorsing the christocentric emphasis that has run throughout the book. Indeed, he may even have had the cross subconsciously at the back of his mind. But herein lies a supreme irony, for the original jazz composition by John Coltrane was originally intended to pull in a quite different direction.

Coltrane had had a very difficult life, including drug addiction, and this piece was planned as his offering to the God who had preserved him through all life's traumas. But, despite his Christian upbringing, it was not of Christ that he was particularly thinking but rather of a universal God operative everywhere.[24] Indeed, his first wife had converted to Islam and he himself repeatedly declared that he thought all religions embodied essentially the same message, that of love. Significantly, in the poem that he wrote to accompany the piece, there is not one mention of Jesus Christ, though plenty of God and his care. Both his parents were children of ministers, and so it is quite likely that the title comes from an influential tract with a similar title by the Scottish minister, Henry Drummond, who had insisted on the priority of love over faith.[25]

It is also such universalism that emerges from the music itself. Coltrane widened the scope of jazz by blending elements of African ritual with Indian and Arabian influences.[26] In the opening section 'Acknowledgement', an Eastern gong leads into a tenor saxophone fanfare that itself yields to the others in the quartet before Coltrane takes up the main four-note figure that is this section's primary theme. At first it appears as a simple bass riff. Later it is heard in the saxophone part and then repeated at different pitches, incorporated into longer melodic phrases, and so forth. If all that sounds boring, it is anything but, as it is subjected to numerous modulations, with frequent changes of key that produce an unsettling but challenging effect. The eventual utterance of the title words that correspond to the four-note figure is in effect unnecessary because through that very variation Coltrane has already informed us that 'God is everywhere – in every register, in every key.'[27] Indeed, in its only publicly performed version, at Antibes, the words were omitted.[28]

So I want to draw a rather different conclusion from that

of Ford – that the deepening of our faith comes not only from within the resources of Christianity but also much more widely, from those of different religious beliefs and sometimes even from those of none. Certainly the glory of God was in the little child at Bethlehem but it was also in the Syrophoenician woman, pagan though she was. Art and music need to be viewed and heard and valued in their own right. The glory of God lies in a love supreme that speaks everywhere, sometimes confirming what we already believe but sometimes too challenging or even undermining what we suppose to be the case. Jesus learnt the value of pagan 'dogs'; can we?[29]

Notes

1 Mark 7:24–30; Matthew 15:21–28 (RSV).
2 Even as distinguished a New Testament scholar as Charles Cranfield insists that the reference is to pet dogs: *The Gospel According to St Mark* (Cambridge: Cambridge University Press, 1977), p. 248.
3 E.g. Isaiah 60:10–14.
4 Austin Farrer, *A Celebration of Faith* (London: Hodder, 1970), pp. 89–90; Rowan Williams, 'The seal of orthodoxy: Mary and the heart of Christian doctrine' in Martin Warner (ed.), *Say Yes to God* (London: Tufton, 1999), pp. 15–29, esp. p. 19.
5 *Tradition and Imagination* (Oxford: Oxford University Press, 1999); *Discipleship and Imagination* (Oxford: Oxford University Press, 2000).
6 O. Toller, *Pfitzner's Palestrina* (London: Toccata Press, 1997), pp. 57, 81–6.
7 Act 1, scenes 5 and 6, especially the latter.
8 John Drury, *Painting the Word* (New Haven: Yale University Press, 1999), esp. pp. 41–59; David Brown, 'The Annunciation as true fiction' in *Theology* 104 (2001), pp. 121–8.
9 Now in Museum Ludwig, Cologne; illustrated in W. Spies (ed.), *Max Ernst: A Retrospective* (Munich: Prestel, 1991), p. 301.
10 The original words of Mrs Alexander's hymn, 'Once in Royal David's City', now commonly changed, as in *The New English Hymnal* (Norwich: Canterbury Press, 1986).
11 E.g. John 12:23, 28; 13:31–2.
12 The painting is in a private collection; illustrated in M. Leiris, *Francis Bacon* (Barcelona: Ediciones Polígrafa, 1987), no. 84.
13 See further D. Farson, *The Gilded Gutter Life of Francis Bacon* (London: Random House, 1994).
14 Based on the phenomenon known as parhelia when two phantom suns are seen either side of the real one.
15 Contrast the Deutsche Grammophon 1979 recording (Barenboim accompanying) with the EMI 1955 one (with Gerald Moore).

16 When interviewed in the BBC DVD version.

17 The Mass in E flat with its mysterious opening *Kyrie*, majestic Gloria, and dramatic symbolism in the Creed.

18 Drury, *Painting the Word*, pp. 155, 147.

19 J. Walker, *John Constable* (London: Thames and Hudson, 1991), no. 26.

20 Owned by Lord Ashton of Hyde; Walker, *John Constable*, no. 37.

21 Both paintings are in the Van Gogh Museum in Amsterdam.

22 In M. T. Benedetti, *Cézanne* (New York: Crescent, 1995), contrast, for example, no. 256 with 258 and 260.

23 D. Ford, *Self and Salvation* (Cambridge: Cambridge University Press, 1999), pp. 280–1.

24 For the background to the album, see A. Kahn, *A Love Supreme* (London: Granta Books, 2002). For his first wife's views, see p. 46, for his own see, for example, introduction, p. xx.

25 Henry Drummond, *Love: The Supreme Gift, the Greatest Thing in the World* (New York: Revell, 1891).

26 V. Wilmer, *As Serious As Your Life: John Coltrane and Beyond* (London: Serpent's Tail, 1992), pp. 32, 36.

27 Lewis Porter cited in Kahn, *A Love Supreme*, p. 102.

28 Interesting also in that improvisation meant that the piece as a whole extended from 33 to 48 minutes.

29 I am grateful to Anne Harrison for her comments on an earlier version of this essay.

4 The Glory of God Revealed in Durham Cathedral: Walking to Prayer

Victor Stock

Meeting at the main entrance outside the door

As the guide book to Durham Cathedral says, 'Not for nothing does the writer Bill Bryson call Durham Cathedral "the finest building on Planet Earth".' The next thing to note from the guide book about the nave is that 'no plans were drawn up for the design of the building; the Master Builder saw in his mind the finished project that he desired and shared his vision with the craftsmen . . . The builder's vision is a metaphor for hope, his skill is a parable of faith and his commitment to seeing the task through to completion is an example of love.' The guide book continues: 'This triad is not a remote theory; faith, hope and love are the three concepts which inform the very way in which people conduct their lives and carry on their work.' Well, that's all very well but we haven't got in yet and I want us to think about the way in which the entrance to this building is not in the obvious place; it's not at the west end, it's well into the nave and at the side. Most of us here in our particular culture approach Christian faith and life 'sideways on'.

When we begin to think about other people in relation to the church – how are we going to get them in – we might reflect on how we got in ourselves, and a building such as this can help us to pray around this. For God is the mysterious 'other' who invites us in very often 'sideways' and unexpectedly, and if that's true for us, it's true for other people coming into the Christian community and into the Christian building. I have often noticed in the City of London people walking around the east end of St Paul's trying to find the way in. Liturgical east and liturgical west and what is to us the perfectly obvious layout of churches are not perfectly obvious to the great majority of human beings on the planet.

Into the nave

My cleaner at Guildford the other day said, 'Are ordinary people allowed in the cathedral?' and it's often been said by all sorts of people about Guildford, 'I often drive along the A3 and see the cathedral, but I've never thought of going in.' When I arrived at Guildford it was quite difficult to get in. The arrangements were to enter by the small north door and then negotiate a set of ropes leading backwards and sideways into the narthex. When I opened the doors at the end of my first week I was asked not to do so again because it made people cold, which, if they insist on sitting near the door, is quite true. Yet the fact of open doors is itself an invitation of some considerable power and is to be heartily recommended.

Here too the extraordinary thing about Durham is not its staggering beauty but that people ignore it. Bill Bryson may think it the finest building on planet earth, but over the years again and again I have passed in the train going north and hardly a person in the compartment has looked out of the window! So as we approach Christian faith and life we need to recognise that what we are doing is not obvious; we often come at it sideways on or stumble across faith through accident. We need time to find the door and to hope that when we have found it it's not locked and that there is a welcome inside, perhaps especially the welcome of silence, space and time.

We kneel

Lord help me to remember now here in the nave how I came into the church, through a parent's faith or practice, through the class or culture or background which took religion for granted, or through my own struggle from a quite alien culture which didn't see the church but passed it by in the train. As I get older and fatter and lazier and less imaginative, help me to enter sympathetically into what it is like to notice the church for the first time and to try to find my way in to it. If I am responsible for worship help me to think on these things at least once a year.

What do I expect people to do with the books I give them at the door, and what do I think people are going to make of the words in the books? Do I give them too many books, Lord? Is it too hard to get in?

We move to the font

We go into this place of faith and power, this place where just by the entrance stands the font, dating from the time of John Cosin, canon here during the reign of Charles I, bishop under Charles II. Two reigns separated by civil war. As Anglicans when we stand by the font there are particular thanksgivings for Cosin and his part in the development of the Book of Common Prayer, for the work he did to beautify the cathedral after the austerity of the Commonwealth, for the recovery after Puritanism of a vibrant and colourful celebration of the joy of God in the faith of the nation.

> Is my faith, Lord, colourful and joyful, immediate and inviting? Does the way the church speaks forward the human flourishing of the nation, the liberation of captives, the setting free of women and men from fear, ignorance and prejudice, or is the church in these days under your judgement?

The Crossing

On page six of the Jarrold Guide to Durham Cathedral there is a picture of the Nave Altar in use, and in more and more of our cathedrals the Nave Altar is the normative place of eucharistic offering around which we gather. When we come to prayer we are always at a place of crossing, the intersection of the timeless with time, and for Christians we are approaching God as we know God to be through the self-offering of Jesus, the Christ of God, at and on the cross. Hence this cathedral, like so many, is itself a cross and we pray within the space made by that cross, a space made by God in the world.

There is much to see around us, which we haven't time to think about much today. The Miners' Memorial back in the nave; that bitter blow when the pits were closed, both to the economy and to the community life of the county – ambivalent feelings there. And there is the Neville Chantry, and the Rose Window, and all those other things that we are going to leave out, like the splendid clock in the South Transept installed by Thomas Castell, Prior of the Community in the fifteenth century.

We are not going to look at the Durham Light Infantry Chapel or at a chapel I remember so well from visits to Michael Ramsey, the Gregory Chapel, where the blessed sacrament is reserved, and where the great retired Bishop of Durham, living just over there in the South Bailey came morning by morning to the Eucharist when he wasn't celebrating it himself in his little chapel at home.

No, here we are at the place of the crossing at the heart of the cathedral, under the tower; height above and space around us, a place for prayer. And always to come to prayer is to discard or leave aside. We can't pray for everybody and we can't be attentive to everything, for if we are we are attentive to nothing and pray for no one. You all know those maddening intercessions where every single misery and sorrow in the world is prayed for and you just sit there counting on your fingers until the end because it's impossible.

Prayer should not be impossible. The church building helps us to be 'at prayer', which is why I hope you might undertake some such exercises as this in your own churches at home. You will begin to see them and feel them in quite different ways if you move about them. In St Mary-le-Bow I would sometimes go down at night when the city was quiet and go into the sanctuary and sit on one of the stalls attached to the east wall and look westward, the opposite way to the way the congregation see the church. Moving around in a sacred building, standing or sitting, kneeling or even lying on the floor, can bring new insights and a new stillness, so here we deliberately ignore much, though we've glanced at it, and that, I think, is the way to deal with distraction in prayer. Let the distractions occupy you for a moment or they will occupy you forever.

You might, for example, if you were praying here and suddenly noticed the clock, ask God to release you for a few minutes from the tyranny of time, or pray for those who are harassed by the passing of time, or those who, on the other hand, want to kill time and then return to the centre, to this place of the cross and the Eucharist, this place of stillness and centredness.

We've been learning in recent years from Hinduism and Buddhism more of the techniques of 'centredness' and they are hugely valuable; centring on that which is most real and therefore centring on God at this place of intersection, of crossing over from the preoccupation of the conscious mind to the work which is so deep down as usually to be unconscious, where God operates in the soul.

That great Bishop of Durham to whom I have just referred, Michael Ramsey, was once asked on television if he prayed every day. 'Oh yes,' he said 'for five minutes.' How terribly shocked the young interviewer looked. 'But I spent fifty-five minutes,' he said 'preparing to pray.' If we didn't rush into worship at the last minute – and priests set a very bad example to people about this – we would find our worship immeasurably deepened.

Let's take that verse of the Psalms we know so well and repeat it now in our minds:

> Be still, and know that I am God.

We walk on up the South Choir Aisle to the Ambulatory and altar behind the High Altar

Paradise

Here we are in Paradise, that place which is beyond the Shrine of St Cuthbert, with Sir Ninian Comper's great gilded tester, added in 1949, where Christ reigns in glory surrounded by the four evangelists. The statue of Cuthbert holds the head of St Oswald, a Christian king who supported the preaching of the gospel in Northumbria, his head resting in the same tomb as Cuthbert's body. And here is Cuthbert himself, that Bishop of Lindisfarne, so famous for his goodness and kindness, whose diocese covered the north-eastern part of England in the second half of the seventh century.

Cuthbert lived the last two years of his life with his community on the Holy Island and was buried there after he died in his solitary hermitage on Inner Farne in 687. Just eleven years after his death his coffin was dug up, so it could be elevated in the sight of the pilgrims. The coffin was opened and the monks were astounded to find, not just bones, but the body of Cuthbert uncorrupted. Soon after Cuthbert's death Viking raids forced the community to leave Lindisfarne carrying Cuthbert's body with them, and they settled here in Durham in 995.

When we pray we are always moving between two worlds: this world and the world which is beyond, or if that language no longer helps, the world which is deeper than the world we are generally conscious of. We enter into paradise, the pleasure park or hunting garden of ancient Persia, the place of refreshment, light and peace, which we ask for the dead, but which we ourselves can experience in prayer.

How valuable it is to have a holy place like the Chapel of the Nine Altars or the Shrine of St Cuthbert, or in Guildford Cathedral, the Lady Chapel hidden beyond the east wall, though in Guildford I wish there were an opening in the east wall, so we could glimpse the beyond. Our worship and prayer needs to glimpse the beyond if it isn't to become wrapped up in self-concern or self-improvement, a bit of pious moralism or a breathing exercise. We need to be open to the winds of the spirit and to all that is beyond metaphor or picture.

Paintings of paradise from different centuries, from the Renaissance to Mark Rothko, illustrate that yearning for Eden, that yearning for a return to the centre which is also a journey as well as a return. 'There we shall rest and we shall see,' says Augustine, 'we shall love and we shall praise in the end that is no end.' And in those wonderful words from the end of the Revelation to John:

Then he showed me the river of the water of life, sparkling like crystal, flowing from the throne of God and of the Lamb down the middle of the city's street. On either side of the river stood a tree of life, which yields twelve crops of fruit, one for each month of the year. The leaves of the tree serve for the healing of the nations, and every accursed thing shall disappear. The throne of God and of the Lamb will be there, and his servants shall worship him; they shall see him face to face, and bear his name on their foreheads. There shall be no more night, nor will they need the light of lamp or sun, for the Lord God will give them light; and they shall reign for evermore. (Rev. 22:1–5, NEB)

And so the twenty-second chapter of the Revelation to John takes us right back to the beginning again, as paradise always must, and we go back to the words of the first chapter:

I turned to see whose voice it was that spoke to me and when I turned I saw seven standing lamps of gold, and among the lamps one like a son of man, robed down to his feet, with a golden girdle round his breast. The hair of his head was white as snow-white wool, and his eyes flamed like fire; his feet gleamed like burnished brass refined in a furnace, and his voice was like the sound of rushing waters. In his right hand he held seven stars, and out of his mouth came a sharp, two-edged sword; and his face shone like the sun in full strength. When I saw him I fell at his feet as though dead. (Rev. 1:12–17, NEB)

We all walk back through the cathedral to the west end and out into the Galilee Chapel

Galilee

Go quickly and tell his disciples that he has risen from the dead, and behold, he is going before you to Galilee, there you will see him . . . So they departed quickly from the tomb, with fear and great joy. (Matt. 28:7–8, RSV)

Matthew points the disciples towards Galilee and in Luke the women who come with him from Galilee followed and

saw the tomb, how his body was laid and then, in the resurrection are told, 'Remember how he told you when he
was still in Galilee' (Luke 24:6).

I wonder if you have any idea why the Galilee Chapel
and the Archbishop of Sydney, Peter Jensen have come
together in my mind. Well, as I was writing this, I heard
Archbishop Jensen, with that kind of terrific smug self-
confidence, saying that the ordination of women wasn't a
bother. It was homosexuality that was going to split the
church apart. And I reflected, knowing the Diocese of
Sydney rather well, that His Grace does not permit women
ordained as priests to function in his diocese, for there they
can only be subservient to men. Women, if priests from other
places, are only permitted to act as deacons. So His Grace
was being a bit economical with the truth there, I thought.

But why Galilee here and Archbishop Jensen? Well,
because years ago they tried to build a Lady Chapel beyond
the east end but St Cuthbert, not liking ladies, wouldn't
have it and that was no good at all. When the building of a
Lady Chapel was begun at the east end of the cathedral, the
foundations were insecure, the walls began to crack. This
was taken as a sign that Cuthbert could not tolerate women
near his shrine, so the Chapel was moved to the west end.

The guide book to the Cathedral says: 'The suggestion
that Cuthbert disliked women is unfounded, for he was on
good terms with, for example, St Hild of Whitby, as well as
other Christian women of his day; it would appear that the
monks may have been attributing their own prejudices to
Cuthbert himself.' All this before the Anglican Communion
was even invented!

No, the Galilee was used as a place of dispersal, of re-
entry into what the Series 2 Eucharist used to call the
world, 'Send us out into the world . . .'. This always
amused me as I wondered where the liturgist thought we'd
been for the last hour. However, here at Durham the great
Sunday Mass ended with the procession to the Galilee, for
Galilee is where Christ goes on before us and meets us. The
Galilee opens us to the world. How marvellous for us to
end our exercise in prayer here, where the historian, the
Venerable Bede, lies buried.

The Venerable Bede was quite a man – he was young

when Cuthbert was bishop. Bede wrote biblical commentaries, works of scientific exploration, and it was largely through his influence that the change in the reckoning of the years was brought about that gave us BC (Before Christ) and AD (Anno Domini – In the Year of Our Lord). His *History of the English Church and People* remains one of our chief sources for the history of the period, and his remains were brought here in 1022. Bede's tomb is simple and the Latin on it simply means: 'In this grave lie the bones of the Venerable Bede.' No grandiloquent epitaph here.

So the Galilee in this cathedral can be the place of re-engagement with the world, but in your own church the door you came in by could serve the same purpose. And when you do this exercise, as I hope you might, at home, getting to know your building and using it for prayer, it's important to make a point of your re-entry, for we've all had experience of going to church on Sunday, or some great feast day, and coming out as if from another planet, wondering where we've been and how what we've just been doing is going to influence our conversations, attitudes and values during the next few days.

I remember preaching on Jeffrey John's appointment as Bishop of Reading on the evening of the day it had been announced that he'd been forced to withdraw. I said to the cathedral congregation at Guildford, 'I'm doing this because I'm reminded of what Alan Webster, then Dean of St Paul's once told me, that on the day Airey Neave was assassinated, no mention was made of it in St Paul's Cathedral.'

To come in at the door, to proceed to the Crossing, to glimpse Paradise, to come to the threshold of Galilee, is to engage for a closer communion, a deeper union, a transformation, a letting in of the light. So let Bede's memorial, his own words, be our last words:

> Christ is the Morning Star, who, when the night of this world is past, brings to his saints the promise of the light of life, and opens everlasting day.

You will find these words on his tomb. I would like them on mine.

5 The Glory of God Revealed in Drama

Michael Hampel

Drama, like the Christian liturgy, glances from heaven to earth, from earth to heaven. Like the liturgy, drama expresses universal truths in the context of temporal things. Like the liturgy, drama encourages its audience to engage in a process of self-examination and lively response as it walks the fine line between the comedy of redemption and the tragedy of hell. The medieval mystery plays, the inevitable William Shakespeare and the revival of religious drama in the early twentieth century provide the stepping stones for this consideration of God's glory revealed in drama. All drama, however, regardless of authorial intention, provides its audience with an opportunity to glimpse this world's destiny.

The experience of sitting in the auditorium of a large theatre is an individual experience. One is conscious of being surrounded by a cloud of witnesses – at least, of a type – but one's concentration is largely exclusive of the fellow members of the audience. The very design of the theatre will often contribute to this particular experience, not to mention the dimming of the lights before curtain up, when one is left feeling strangely alone despite the occasional shuffling around of someone nearby and the sadly not so occasional coughing.

When one attends a performance at a proscenium arch theatre, it is worth taking the opportunity perhaps during the interval to wander down to the front of the stalls and look back. In one of the great theatres, like the Royal Shakespeare Theatre at Stratford, it is in its own way a stunning sight. Not only is the space vast but the sudden realisation that one is indeed in the company of some thousand or so fellow spectators may change one's experience of the drama for good and turn it in a more fruitful direction.

This is because the experience of the drama should be at once individual and corporate if it is to be a true experience of drama. There is nothing passive about membership of an audience – or at least there should not be. No actor, taking a night off and finding himself part of an audience for once, would ever regard his activity in the audience as passive. When actors talk of a 'responsive audience', they are not merely appraising the degree of laughter or applause. Actors sense responsive audiences even in the silence.

Religious drama, inasmuch as there is such a thing, is perhaps most obviously typified by the great mystery plays of the middle ages when biblical stories were placed upon the stage for edification and, increasingly, for entertainment too. God's glory was not so much revealed by this drama as proved by it in a didactic exercise which, along with stained-glass windows and architecture, pointed to God in his heaven rather than revealed him in his world.

The medieval mystery or miracle or morality plays painted vivid pictures of biblical, hagiographical and ethical stories as a means of communicating church doctrine to the 'ordinary' people. The earliest origins of the form lie in the attempts by members of monastic communities to interpret the themes of the liturgy for the people who were unable to understand the Latin texts of the liturgy itself. As they gradually abandoned this process, the medieval guilds assimilated the project for themselves and the performances thrived while, at the same time, acquiring greater wit and humour than had originally been intended. The very designation of 'mystery' plays derives from the 'mestier' or 'metier' of the members of each guild.

The involvement of the craft guilds meant that the dramatic performances were accomplished in a utilitarian manner with the people of the local community and their market place or their church or both providing the raw materials for their stagecraft. There was certainly no playhouse, no proscenium arch, nor stalls within or before which to articulate the traffic of the stage. It was not a sophisticated operation. Likewise, the poetry of the medium was not a sophisticated communication of language but rather a means of emphasising both the sublimity and the humility of what the people were witnessing. The sound of the words was intended to underline the action of what was happening while the rhyming couplets exalted that meaning above the ordinary nature of daily lives. Hence, the union of time and eternity was accomplished while the relationship between God and men and women was brought sharply into focus. The doctrine of the incarnation which underlies the dramatic tradition of the mystery plays draws the past into the present and 'weds' earth to heaven. By developing this concept, the dramatist also weds the employment of actual people and events to the articulation of universal and enduring ideas. This is the sacramental aesthetic which connects creative activity to the work of the Master Maker.

And it is this union of time and eternity which all art articulates but which drama stretches almost to its limits. Drama places the doctrine of the incarnation on the stage where it is played out in the flesh and blood of the men and women whom we call actors. But unless the audience itself reaches beyond the imaginary screen which, together with the proscenium arch, appears to separate auditorium from stage, the sacramental aesthetic will have little or no effect upon it. It is not enough for the actor to play through that so-called screen if the audience does not respond through it. The outward and visible form cannot reveal the inward and spiritual truth if it has no impact on the audience.

The implications for God's glory not being revealed in drama because of a passive audience are similar to the implications for the liturgy of a passive congregation. The concept of the whole congregation celebrating the Eucharist with one person presiding or performing the actions on behalf of the congregation is similar to that of the actors in a play presenting the audience with a glimpse of its own destiny – and all of this within the context of the dramatic unities and indeed what we might call the liturgical unities. After all, the very useful classical unities of time, place and action are worth observing in both contexts: the Thirty Years War cannot be presented on the stage in three hours any more than a church service can say everything there is to say about God in one hour (despite the attempts of certain earnest clerics to do just that).

So, what about these universal and enduring ideas which the dramatist seeks to articulate through his or her stagecraft? The great theatrical masks of comedy and tragedy perhaps provide a neat epitome of the narrow path between redemption and self-destruction which is the never-ending avenue along which all drama is propelled, be it through the great productions of the Royal Shakespeare Company or the weekly menus of the soap operas on television.

Tragedy in drama is the playing out of a story which draws to its close without the redemption of its central character. The anti-hero – the Macbeth or the Othello of Shakespeare, for example – does not look back upon a life resolved or reconstituted when the curtain falls for the last time. 'It doth follow as the night the day' that he will die and that there will be no resurrection through which to transmogrify the envy, malice, betrayal, lies, pride and mis-understanding of the character whose lifetime we have glimpsed for the previous few hours.

And here are those qualities again, this time played out by Shakespeare's tragic heroes: the envy of Iago shown towards Othello; the malice of Hamlet against Claudius; the betrayal by Richard III of his brother Clarence; the lies of Macbeth to his guests; the pride of Julius Caesar which causes his downfall; the misunderstanding by King Lear of his daughter's loyalty. Sin without the possibility of redemption destroys utterly. Let the *audience* look to its conscience.

But we knew about that already. Here is the gospels' take on the same qualities: the envy of Jesus' disciples when they argue about status; the malice of the religious leaders towards Jesus; the betrayal by Judas of his Saviour; the lies of Peter about his relationship with Jesus; the pride of Pontius Pilate creating deadlock over Jesus' fate; the mis-understanding by Thomas of the identity of the risen Christ. That is their tragedy and, for three particular days, it is our tragedy as the curtain hangs limply over the scene of our own envy, malice, betrayal, lies, pride and misun-derstanding. Let the *congregation* look to its conscience.

The house is dark: the sickly sweet tinge of grease-paint lingers on the air, the echo of that final speech reverberates no more, the audience has gone. So it must have been in that other theatre 2000 years ago – that bare, rude stage of a stone tomb hewn out of a rock. That playhouse, in which our own destinies were dramatised by the greatest player of them all, was dark; no grease-paint but the similar aroma of oils and spices; the prosaic grinding of the stone boulder into place the only soliloquy; the audience, in this case, not only gone away but run away. Tragedy. Not a Shakespearean tragedy though because, in a Shakespearean tragedy, the central character is the cause of his own downfall. Here, the tragedy is deeper, more profound, more pathetic. Here, the central character, Jesus, the Son of God, the one whom God sent, the light to lighten the Gentiles, and the glory of God's people Israel, here, his own downfall is caused by everyone else. That is why it is *our* tragedy.

But Shakespeare, of course, wrote other plays. We call them comedies: not comedies like those television comedies which amuse us and make us laugh. The denouement of these dramas is characterised by a resolving or a redeeming of all that has been unresolved or unredeemed during the course of the play. We may indeed be encouraged to laugh in a Shakespearean comedy and thank God for that. Laughter is good for the soul. What we are particularly encouraged to do in a Shakespearean comedy, however, is to examine ourselves closely and to discover ways of repenting; of making good that which is lacking in us; of shedding anything which denies both to ourselves and to those around us the possibility of new opportunities and fresh starts.

In a Shakespearean comedy, there is always someone who is not quite what he seems. This person's role in the drama is a catalyst to encourage this process of self-examination and call to repentance which ultimately sets people free – to be more fully human and thus more fully alive. In *As You Like It*, Rosalind disguises herself as a young man in order to retrieve her wronged father, the deposed Duke, and restore him to his rule. In the course of her endeavours, she finds love for herself in the character of Orlando. Her cousin Celia through her own love for

Orlando's charlatan brother Oliver, manages to transform him from heartless rogue into romantic husband, as well as effect a reconciliation between the two brothers. In *Measure for Measure*, the Duke, disturbed by the lapse in moral standards in his dukedom and the abuse of power amongst his officials, disguises himself as a friar in order to place himself unobserved in the midst of his people and strip the veil of seeming from the hypocrites and double-dealers of society. In *The Winter's Tale*, the jealousy of Leontes is abated and dissolved by his wife Hermione. She makes a pretence of death until her husband has fully repented of his treatment of her before she returns to his side in a *coup de grâce* possibly unequalled in the canon. In *The Taming of the Shrew*, Petruchio makes a play of treating Katherine in precisely the same manner in which she has behaved towards her family and friends until she reconsiders her attitude and becomes the amiable wife and dutiful daughter with whom it is henceforth a delight to live. And so one could continue.

Little wonder then that so many parallels have been drawn between drama *per se* and the greatest drama ever staged. I suggested above that drama encourages its audience to engage in a process of self-examination and lively response. And certainly both Shakespeare's tragedies and his comedies encourage the process of self-examination. What of the lively response? Perhaps one of the great difficulties in discerning God's glory revealed in drama is a failure on the part of so many people to see much drama in the story of humankind's redemption in the first place. The familiar story has been so dissected and tossed around, so sifted and weighed, that it has lost its dynamism and therefore its appeal. It no longer elicits a lively response.

One sees the reason for people's failure to appreciate the drama inherent in the biblical accounts both in church and theatre. In church, there is a sense in which we have turned Christ into what Dorothy L. Sayers has called 'a household pet for pale curates and pious old ladies'. Now, when Dorothy L. Sayers said this, she was speaking as a dramatist. From 1937, at the height of the revival of religious drama in churches and theatres, she produced several significant dramas on religious themes and is best remembered for her cycle of radio plays on the life of Christ, *The Man Born to be King*. When Sayers describes Christ, she does so with the eye of the dramatist: out for a good story, after a character who will command the attention of an audience, mindful of her technique. When she speaks of 'that shattering personality', we hear a master of stagecraft seizing an opportunity to place the central character in the Christian drama in the limelight – literally. Of the doctrine of the incarnation, Sayers wrote, 'Now, we may call that doctrine exhilarating or we may call it devastating; we may call it revelation or we may call it rubbish; but if we call it dull, then words have no meaning at all.'[1] And yet, by comparison with the English Touring Theatre's production of *King Lear* at Durham's new Gala Theatre in 2002, the presentation of the greatest drama that ever staggered the human imagination is, in most churches, just that – dull.

And then, in the theatre, the very idea of a religious play about Jesus dampens any enthusiasm for the stage which actors should ordinarily possess. It is hard work making an actor play Jesus as if he really was ever a fully human being. Sayers again: 'At the name of Jesus, every voice goes plummy, every gesture becomes pontifical, and a fearful creeping paralysis slows down the pace of the dialogue.'[2]

Christ in the drama then sets off to a bad start. And there are two reasons for this: one is that we fail to explore Christianity's universal and enduring ideas either in the existing dramatic repertoire or by commissioning new works from established playwrights and the other is that, when we do put Christ onto the stage in our churches through the liturgy, we make do with second best. This effectively means making do with poor quality drama. Loose and sentimental drama leads to loose and sentimental theology. And yet Sayers has said, 'There is no more searching test of a theology than to submit it to dramatic handling.'[3]

The most significant of Sayers' contemporaries in the religious drama movement of the 1930s and 1940s is T. S. Eliot. In his essay 'A Dialogue on Dramatic Poetry', one of his interlocutors in the dialogue argues that the issue about drama is one of form and suggests that the future of drama (and he is talking principally of poetic drama) may lie in

the direction indicated by ballet. This is because the expo-
nent of that particular form, that is the dancer, has under-
gone a rigorous physical training akin to the refining nature
of a moral training and unlike the experience of a contemporary actor. Such an argument would be hotly disputed
by actors contemporary with Eliot and indeed with our
own time. Sayers in *The Mind of the Maker* states categori-
cally that she prefers the rigorous physical qualities of the
actor to any great concern about his moral qualities. She is
responding to a question about whether she chooses the
actors in her religious dramas for their moral qualities or
not. In Eliot's 'Dialogue', another interlocutor concludes
that the reason why his colleagues approve the analogy
with the ballet is because it alone of dramatic forms is
expressed through a 'system of physical training, of traditional, symbolical and highly skilled movements'.[4] He then
uses a related analogy or, at least, an analogy which he
chooses to relate to the ballet – that of the liturgy:

> I say that the consummation of the drama, the perfect and ideal
> drama, is to be found in the ceremony of the Mass. I say ... that
> drama springs from religious liturgy, and that it cannot afford
> to depart far from religious liturgy ... [W]hen drama has
> ranged as far as it has in our own day, is not the only solution
> to return to religious liturgy? And the only dramatic satisfac-
> tion that I find now is in a High Mass well performed. And
> indeed, if you consider the ritual of the Church during the cycle
> of the year, you have the complete drama represented. The
> Mass is a small drama, having all the unities; but in the Church
> year you have represented the full drama of creation.[5]

However, this argument is only fully supportable if it is
based on a relationship between religion and drama and
not on any possibility of substituting the one for the other.
In other words, going to the theatre is hardly a substitute
for going to church and the best drama will not, as we have
suggested, necessarily be found in church. Many people
may enjoy a High Mass well performed as a work of art
without possessing any religious sensibilities or being concerned about the meaning of the celebration. Equally, other
people will flee religion and find a substitute for inveterate
sensibilities in the pages of literature.

However, the several commentators who have drawn analogies between drama and liturgy are not stretching a point. There are analogies to be drawn at several levels, not least between the responsive audience of the theatre and the responsive congregation at the Eucharist. Think, for example, of the 'sursum corda'. A responsive audience is an active and not a passive audience. Only an active congregation may lift up its hearts in order to be able to participate in the celebration of the Eucharist. Herbert Coursen, in the introduction to his treatment of Christian ritual and Shakespearean tragedy, writes about the communion as comedy: 'The importance of the moment of Communion for the Elizabethan cannot be overemphasised, for it is in the receiving of the sacraments and not in the consecration of the elements that the fusion of Christ and communicant, blood and wine occurs.'[6] This is the moment when the participant may make a physical response to the drama of the Mass: the movement to the altar, the genuflecting, the crossing of oneself, the holding out of hands, and so on. It is, in its own way, a highly symbolic mime of redemption. And, just as the mass must be 'answered', so a dramatic performance in the theatre must be 'responded to' if the sacramental aesthetic is to have any meaning.

So, if God's glory is revealed in drama, it may be revealed in the same way that it is revealed in liturgy: by creating a scene in which the eternal and the temporal are fused in a constant acting out of the nativity, the incarnation. Consider, for example, the incarnational undercurrent of the medieval mystery plays where divine and human reality were married in a pithy and earthy folk drama in which spectators were surely encouraged to regard themselves as participants.

The incarnation reveals the nature of eternity to us. The possibility that drama expresses the fusion of eternity and history not only draws this inevitable comparison with the medieval mystery plays but, perhaps more importantly, teaches the doctrine in the context of human reality, reminding men and women that they are not mere spectators of a nativity in Bethlehem but also active participants in the life of Christ in their own day.

This rediscovery of the importance of the doctrine of the

incarnation in dramatic form is the backdrop against which the likes of T. S. Eliot and Dorothy L. Sayers as well as many other writers in the particularly fertile period of the 1930s and 1940s make their own contribution to religious drama. They do so because of what William Spanos calls 'this incarnational bent of Anglican theology', a bent which, he says, 'goes far to illuminate the strategies that Eliot and the other dramatists of the movement evolved to confront and dramatise the discontinuities of contemporary history'.[7] Thus he emphasises the Anglican affiliation of the principal participants in the movement as being no mere coincidence. At the same time, albeit rather indirectly, he makes a connection with the growing unrest of European society in the years immediately preceding the Second World War when he refers to 'the dissociated sensibility and the anarchy of the experience of modern life'.[8]

Thus life had been sanctified by the incarnation such that each element of it, human and natural, was real and universal. The humble and the sublime had been merged through Christ's incarnation and passion. The relationship between spirit and matter changed because, despite their being unhappy bedfellows throughout much of church history, the incarnation fused spirit and matter. And the point relevant to this argument is that a proper understanding of this new relationship was being seized upon by the dramatist. He or she could more readily employ 'real things' to express universal truths without compromising either the reality of the thing itself or dissolving the significance of the universal truth to which it pointed. Interestingly enough, Dorothy L. Sayers argues for a reappraisal by the church of the relationship between spirit and matter in her essay 'Towards a Christian Aesthetic' in which she criticises the church for presiding over a divorce of spirit and matter, suggesting that the church has dislocated its patronage of the arts from its theology of the arts. She also uses the example of dramatic form to draw an analogy between Christ as both the image of the Father and one and the same with the Father against a play as the expression of something happening in the mind of the writer but only known to the writer by the process of expressing it in written form.[9]

It is only fair to admit, however, that little of the work produced during this early twentieth century revival in religious drama has survived in the popular memory. The one great exception to this is T. S. Eliot's *Murder in the Cathedral* of 1935. Nevertheless, even the 'Master' was inclined to be slightly dismissive of this particular dramatic work, certainly in comparison with the plays he wrote for the commercial theatre. He maintained that this play, written for the Canterbury Festival of 1935, had been written in a very particular context for a very particular audience who 'go to Festivals and expect to have to put up with poetry'.[10]

Now it is possible that the obstacles above which the presentation of religious drama needed to rise in its day have amassed once more to confirm a later generation in its disregard for such drama. There was a sense then, surely shared today, that religious drama was a means of 'tricking' people into attending church.[11] At the same time, professional writers needed to be convinced that the label of 'religious dramatist' would not impose a death warrant.[12] But I hope that I have indicated that the drama is not obliged to be religious for the sacramental aesthetic to be effective. The Lord of Creation is not to be banished from any of his own dominions.

When in 1935 *Murder in the Cathedral* was staged in the Chapter House at Canterbury, the Friends of Canterbury Cathedral, who promoted the Festival, did more than exercise patronage on an existing playwright. They, perhaps inadvertently, inspired a significant development in Eliot's own artistic journey as he moved from the tentative dramatic effort of his *Sweeney Agonistes* past the pageant-style production of *The Rock* to the beginning of his psychological dramas in which the reintroduction of the chorus as a vital dramatic tool in his stagecraft would itself develop in a remarkable and creative manner. This is the point at which certain playwrights were forced to give serious thought to the genre they were being encouraged to pursue. Did they know that they were contributing to a developmental period in British drama which would not encounter another watershed until Samuel Beckett and

John Osborne a generation later? Kenneth Pickering, in his analysis of the history of the Canterbury Festival, writes:

> Had Eliot written no other play, his reputation as a dramatist would have been established and had the Canterbury Festival produced no further commissions after 1935 it would still be entitled to claim its part in a revolution in the English Theatre.[13]

Consider the shock experienced by those who attended the first night in 1935 when the four knights turned to the audience and proceeded to excuse what they had done by implicating the audience itself in the murderous deed just carried out before them. This changed the whole concept of the audience being merely a passive witness to the transpositions of stage drama. Never before had the sacramental aesthetic which traduces eternity in a single moment in art been so beautifully articulated by the physical turn of an actor on stage. Anyone who has attended a dramatic performance at which a member of the cast has suddenly addressed the audience directly and, perhaps for that purpose, the house lights have been raised, will know something of the slight tingle down the spine which one experiences on such an occasion. If one was in any doubt about the degree of one's participation in the drama, this experience removes it. And yet it is merely an expression of the process of self-examination and lively response which should attend all drama.

The revelation of God's glory in drama turns the spotlight on us over and over again – perhaps when we are least expecting it. Like the tragedy and comedy of the stage, the leading character in the greatest drama ever staged came amongst us in the guise of a human being – not quite what he seemed – in fact, far more than what he seemed: God, our God. Both the principal player in our lives and the chief spectator of them. The sealed tomb was not the final playing out of a tragedy. It was merely the interval, the intermission, the break – waiting for the resolution of the plot, the redemption of those who had destroyed the leading character; waiting, in other words, for the resurrection.

The house is not dark; the tinge on the air is the sweet smell of life in all its fullness; the auditorium of this world is full of the speeches of men and women and children playing their part and making their entrances and their exits upon the stage of life; the seats are not empty but instead are filled with the great cloud of witnesses which surrounds us and which we shall join in time when we take the final curtain.

I have tried to draw an analogy between drama and liturgy by articulating the sacramental aesthetic implicit in both and by emphasising the importance of the participation of the audience and congregation in a process of self-examination and lively response. All of these aspects of my argument are themselves articulated and emphasised by the doctrine of the incarnation. That doctrine placed Christ upon the stage and ever since has enabled the stage to run the never-ending performance of the outward and visible form of the theatre pointing to the inward and spiritual truth of God for the benefit of the outward and visible form of the audience on its inward and spiritual journey.

Notes

1 Dorothy L. Sayers, *The Greatest Drama Ever Staged* (London: Hodder and Stoughton, 1938), p. 22.
2 Sayers, 'Divine Comedy' in *Unpopular Opinions: Twenty-one Essays* (London: Victor Gollancz, 1946), pp. 20–1.
3 Sayers, *The Man Born to be King* (London: Victor Gollancz, 1945), p. 19.
4 T. S. Eliot, 'A Dialogue on Dramatic Poetry' (1932) in *Selected Essays* (London: Faber and Faber, 1951), p. 47.
5 ibid.
6 Herbert R. Coursen Jr, *Christian Ritual and the World of Shakespeare's Tragedies* (Lewisburg: Bucknell University Press, 1976), p. 19.
7 William V. Spanos, *The Christian Tradition in Modern British Verse Drama: The Poetics of Sacramental Time* (New Jersey: Rutgers University Press, 1967), p. 25.
8 ibid., p. 26
9 Sayers, 'Towards a Christian Aesthetic' in *Unpopular Opinions*, pp. 29–43.
10 Eliot, 'Poetry and Drama' in *Selected Prose* (London: Faber and Faber, 1975), p. 139.
11 See Denis Donoghue, *The Third Voice* (Princeton: Princeton University Press, 1959), p. 158; cited in Arnold Hinchliffe, 'Verse Drama', *British Theatre 1950–1970* (Oxford: Blackwell, 1974), p. 39.
12 Ivor Brown refers to 'The Crypt of St Eliot's', cited in Katherine Worth, 'Eliot and the Living Theatre' in Graham Martin (ed.), *Eliot in Perspective: A Symposium* (London: Macmillan, 1970), p. 148.

13 Kenneth Pickering, *Drama in the Cathedral: The Canterbury Festival Plays, 1928–1948*, (Worthing: Churchman in association with the Friends of Canterbury Cathedral, 1985), p. 178.

6 The Glory of God Revealed in 'Genuine' Celtic Spirituality

Kate Tristram

I must begin with an explanation of my title for the talk. It is not that I, an Englishwoman without a drop of Celtic blood in me, am conceited enough to think that I can tell you what 'genuine' Celtic spirituality is.[1] But I have met so much that I am convinced is not genuine and the reason for that is the place where I live. Twenty-five years ago I moved from Durham to the Holy Island of Lindisfarne. I am the kind of person who would always be interested in the place where I lived, so I read up all that I could find about our first monastery on the island, and in due course fell in love with the Irish monks and the Christian tradition they brought. I tried to develop this during the years and when I retired from my main job there five years ago I went to the University of Edinburgh part-time for two years to do their MSc course in medieval language, choosing as my two languages medieval Latin and Old Irish, which would have been those used by our early monks. I thought that if I could learn their languages I might be able to enter better into their thought and I am hoping to pursue that study further.

During my years on the island, continuing to read, but also to talk to innumerable groups of visitors, I have become aware of notions about Celtic spirituality which to me are distortions of the real thing. These have seemed to be based on two mistaken lines of thought. The first is a need to impose our own agenda and find answers to our own problems in this ancient material, and when I say 'ancient material' I am thinking specially of that which comes from the first five or so centuries of Christian faith in Ireland, because that is what I know best. The second mistake is a certain romanticism of approach, a kind of nostalgia for that which never was. There are people who seem to think it would be rather charming to live on Holy Island in a little wooden hut in winter! Even those of us who live in our little stone huts with all mod cons sometimes find the place a bit bleak, especially if a breeze is blowing at 140 miles an hour, which has been recorded.

Let me give some examples of what I mean. Our conference this weekend is concerned with the creation and many people hold that the Celtic monks were particularly interested in nature. In support of this I have seen quoted in many of the smaller books on Celtic spirituality a single sentence from the writing of the Irish monk Columbanus. He is important in that he is possibly our earliest authentic Irish Christian voice, and his writings our earliest evidence for Irish monasticism. He was born somewhere around 550, was a monk at Bangor in northern Ireland until his forties, and then felt God's call to become a pilgrim. He travelled across southern Europe, founding monasteries, making enemies and friends, until he founded his last monastery at Bobbio in the north of Italy, where he died in 615. From him have survived a number of writings, including a sequence of 13 sermons, probably preached to his own monks in the last year of his life. The much-quoted sentence comes in Sermon 1: 'Understand the creation, if you wish to know the Creator.'[2] I have seen it quoted many times, but have never seen it placed in context. If we do that I think we see it differently. Columbanus is not saying to his monks, 'Go out and do a bit of nature-study.' Rather he is saying, 'Stop prattling ignorantly about God.' His point is that his monks do not and cannot understand nature; how much less can they presume to speak about the mysteries of God. He seems to stand here in the tradition that was developed later by *The Cloud of Unknowing*, when the human being realises how totally human language fails when confronted with the divine. For instance, the author of *The Cloud* writes 'by love can he be gotten and holden, but by thought – never!' Columbanus indeed allows nature to point to the greatness of God, as when he writes: 'High is the heaven, broad the earth, deep the sea, and long the ages; but higher and broader and deeper and longer is the knowledge of him who created nature out of nothing.' It seems to me that this earliest Celtic Christian would allow nature to impress us with God's majesty, as St Paul does. But what interests Columbanus, what his writings are really about, is the Christian life, the life of obedience which is pleasing to God.

My point there, and it may seem a small one to you, is that there is a misuse of evidence when something is taken out of context and made to fit into a modern conception of Celtic Christianity. Let me give another example of the sort of thing I find worrying. It's the way people deal with the Synod of Whitby. You will know that this was a meeting called by King Oswy of Northumbria in 664, basically to decide whether his kingdom should continue to follow the religious leadership of Iona, or whether it should, so to speak, turn round and face the continent. The debate centred on matters of controversy, such as the method of calculating the date of Easter, and ended with the King's decision to turn to the continent. To me, given all the circumstances, that decision seems both inevitable and right. But so many people look upon it as some kind of catastrophe, a defeat for Celtic Christianity, caricatured as free and creative, by the Roman church, caricatured as hidebound and authoritarian. Neither picture seems to me to fit the facts. But on the Island I get asked again and again, right up to this week in fact, to explain the differences between good Celtic Christianity and bad Roman Christianity. If I try to explain that this is mistaken, that for example our early writer Columbanus expresses gratitude to Rome for sending the faith, they get disgusted. One man from the United States said to me recently that they had a great body of material over there on this Celtic/Roman thing. I think he meant a large number of popular books. I can well believe it. But I still think it is a mistake.

The imposing of a modern agenda goes on. Take, for instance, the position of women. I am told they had equality. It seems that in sober fact women did not even have legal status in Ireland. Now of course it is possible for a culture to have a respect for women, apart from any question of law. Perhaps Ireland did not have the contempt for women of some Mediterranean lands. Perhaps the same is true of Anglo-Saxon England, as the historian Stenton thought. But when people tell me that St Brigid was consecrated as a bishop I fall into despair. And when I tell them that perhaps there was no such person as St Brigid, they seem for some reason to get angry. One man said to me furiously once, 'Would you go to Kildare and say that?' Well, of course.

On this basis it is now time to turn to the attitude to 'nature'. The spiritual tradition the Irish monks inherited, from the Desert Fathers on, shows two ways of responding to the beauty of nature. Many years ago I was privileged to belong to a group which was scrambling over the Sinai range of hills. Our leader was a lecturer from the University of Jerusalem, an archaeologist whose life's work had been a study of those mountains during the early Christian centuries, when, he said, they had been inhabited by possibly thousands of hermits. He led us to large numbers of the sites he had investigated, where these Desert Fathers had lived. He showed us the caves and also the ledges on which they perched. He showed us the leopard traps, still working, though there are no longer any leopards, and the little gardens in the valleys still cultivated by the Bedouin. I was enthralled by it all but I remember particularly that he said there was one persistent feature when the hermits chose their sites: whether ledge or cave, they all looked out on a view of dazzling natural beauty and that, he thought, could hardly be accidental. One imagines them singing their psalms and gazing.

But there were those who responded differently, who denied themselves this beauty in order to concentrate on the life of prayer. I remember the story of a Desert Mother, who lived for 20 years beside a river, and never once looked down into it. And if your first reaction to that is the same as mine, namely 'what a waste of a good river', that simply shows how foreign such a way of thinking has become to us. Yet, much nearer to home, it needs to be borne in mind that our very own St Cuthbert, when he built his hermitage on the Inner Farne, surrounded it by a high wall so that, according to Bede, 'he could see nothing except the sky from his dwelling, thus restraining both the lust of the eyes and of the thoughts and lifting the whole bent of his mind to higher things'[3] and increasingly, as the years went by, he spent his time inside the hermitage and not outside on the island. Well, we already knew that the purpose of the hermit was not peace and quiet. We did not think that St Cuthbert went to the Inner Farne for 10 years to have a good rest! The purpose of the hermit was to engage in deadly combat with the greatest enemy of all, the spiritual forces of evil, to win spiritual victories, through his prayer and loyalty, which then would spread out as benefits to the whole church. So when we hear of Irish monks going out to 'seek a desert' in the forests or in the seas, idyllic as it may sound to us, we must realise that they were really seeking a place of battle, which might end only with their own death in that place. While there is some lovely, peaceful nature poetry from Ireland, which used to be called 'hermit poetry', it is not now attributed to hermits. The real hermits were too busy with their fighting.

But the hermits of course were specialists, God's crack troops, his front-line soldiers, and they were always very few in number, compared with the large numbers of other monks and nuns, and all the secular Christians. So can we say anything about these, their attitudes to 'nature', and whether these attitudes were different from those of other early medieval Western Christians?

The first point, obvious as it is, is that nature to them was natural: 'natural' in a way that I think it can't be any longer to us. They would not have made a distinction between nature and themselves. Perhaps it is a characteristic of city-dwellers to do this, to think of 'nature' as something one finds in the country as distinct from the city. But of course the Irish, having escaped the Roman Empire, had no cities, no towns, and made no such distinction. As farmers, mainly cattle-farmers, they were constantly aware of the forces of nature. Even their great heroic epics took the outward form of cattle-raids. Nature was simply where they lived and so they did not define it. I am reminded of a friend who was studying sacrifice in the ancient world. He believed that he had read all the sources available to him, but there was one thing he had never found: a definition of sacrifice. It was, he said, too much just part of life: everyone knew what sacrifice was and meant.

So nature was natural, but it was a creation. It was all the product of a single divine mind, and it was all owned by a single divine being. So the Christian faith taught them and some historians of pagan Ireland have thought that the Irish would not have found this difficult, because their type of paganism had intuited, behind the stories of a multiplicity of gods and spirits, a unity of living beings, the sense of a life-force flowing through all. And certainly the Genesis stories took a firm hold. But creation, of course, meant that the whole world is God's possession. Nothing is ours to do whatever we like with.

But if everything is God's then he can use it, especially physical things to convey spiritual lessons. For example, there is the story of St Chad and the thunderstorm.[4] Although Chad was English he was thoroughly Irish in training. He had been a boy in St Aidan's little school on Lindisfarne and, because he was academically gifted, Aidan had sent him for further education to some of the great monasteries in Ireland itself. When he returned, after several years' study there, he was possibly, in the Irish method, the most highly educated person in the north of England. He became briefly Bishop of York and then missionary bishop in Mercia. His monks noticed his behaviour in a thunderstorm. At the first indication of a storm Chad would stop what he was doing and begin to pray, especially for God's mercy on the human race. As the storm got worse he prayed more earnestly; if it became really violent he entered his chapel and prayed concentratedly until the storm stopped. His monks had no reason to think that he was more afraid of thunder than most of us are, so they asked him why he did this. His reply was that the Lord was the author of the storm and that it provided a heaven sent opportunity for humans to meditate on something equally certain and far more dangerous, namely, the Day of Judgement. Both realities, physical and spiritual, came from the same God, who was not split-minded; one could be used therefore to remind us of the other.

At this point I would like to put in something which might seem like a digression but is in fact central: the

devotion of the Irish to biblical study. I have read that, if
you had been able to stop in the street a well-informed person on the continent in the seventh century and ask him
what Irish monks were good at, he would have replied,
'asceticism and Bible study'. As far as asceticism goes, it is
important to note that they were vigorous in the use of normal ascetic practices, such as fasting, and that the Irish
practice of leaving home to go 'on pilgrimage for Christ' is
perhaps best understood as a branch of asceticism. But
about biblical study they were passionate. When
Christianity came to Ireland it brought with it the new arts
of reading and writing, for Irish pagan culture, though put-
ting a high value on learning had been, except for a form of
inscriptive writing, non-literate. The books brought by the
Christian faith were all in Latin including Latin versions of
the books of the Bible. No one quite knows how they did it,
but the Irish set to work to learn Latin, and succeeded
astonishingly, as their early Latin writings show. Biblical
study appears to have been their favourite department of
Christian learning. They considered themselves doctrinally
orthodox but they seem not to have cared for the niceties of
doctrinal or philosophical discussion. The really important
thing in life was to discover the will of God and obey it. So
their Bible study was practical, approached with the question: 'How does God want us to live?' Then they went out
to live like that. As well as the Psalms and the gospels they
particularly liked the wisdom literature and the moral laws
of the Old Testament. Perhaps they would strike us as
legalistic, and certainly some scholars have thought them
Pelagian, over-interested in the immense effort required of
humans to live in obedience to God.

Perhaps, with that background, it is not surprising that
in some of the earliest Irish Christian poetry that we have,
'nature' appears as nature in the biblical revelation rather
than as the nature we see all around us. For example, an
early poem from Iona, so early that some have thought that
it comes from the great St Columba himself, is known by its
first two Latin words 'Altus Prosator', 'the high creator'.[5]
The poem describes at length the creation in its various
levels, the apocryphal fall of Lucifer and the demons, the
fall of man and the reality of hell; then it mentions briefly

the Sinai covenant and moves straight on to the Last Judgement conceived in most terrifying terms. The only mention of Christ is as Judge at his Second Coming. The imagery is biblical throughout but a recent editor has remarked 'There was something lacking in a long poem where mercy and tenderness, the humility and patience of God with sinful humanity, are not mentioned once.'[6] But if we doubted the toughness – almost the ferocity – of some of the earliest Irish Christianity, we might read this poem and doubt it no longer.

Of course this kind of thing is not the only poetry from Christian Ireland, though it belongs to the earliest that we know. Other early poems, especially those connected with Iona include, as one might expect, praise-poems about the great founder, Columba himself, and perhaps these reflect similar praise-poetry from pagan days. If we turn to another very early writer, who had nothing at all to do with Iona, Columbanus, we find that he also wrote poetry. But critical study of those works attributed to him have narrowed his authentic poems down to two at the most: of these, one is an Easter hymn similar to the Exsultet and the other seems to be an invitation to young men to choose the monastic life, so neither is a nature poem. Although it is usually dated from a later period we do indeed find some serene nature poetry, like this little gem:

> Over my head the woodland wall
> Rises; the blackbird sings to me.
> Above my booklet lined for words
> The woodland birds shake out their glee.
> There's the blithe cuckoo chanting clear
> In mantle grey from bough to bough.
> God keep me still! For here I write
> A scripture bright in great woods now.[7]

Is this, we might ask, a hermit poem? Or a monk who, on a fine day, has moved his writing table a few yards from his well-ordered monastery into its pleasant garden? Or even an armchair naturalist, since cuckoos in fact don't chant as they go from bough to bough? Poetry can so often express visions and dreams: it doesn't always lead us directly to an actual situation.

We move on from the poetry tradition to the prayer tradition. I am not now dealing with the prayers from the Hebrides, as gathered in the collection called *Carmina Gadelica*. They are of course Celtic, but come from a completely different background.[8] From ancient Ireland two kinds of prayers stand out. There are the breastplate prayers, of which the best-known is the one called St Patrick's Breastplate, which in our hymnbooks begins with the words 'I bind unto myself today'[9] and there are other examples.[10] The second kind is the litany and Irish litanies have come down to us consisting of pages and pages of invocations of every saint that exists and, one suspects, several that don't. Saint so-and-so, pray for me, or us. Behind both these types of prayer is a realistic sense of the fragility of the human being, the need for protection and help. For nature, as well as one's fellow humans, could wreak sudden havoc and destruction. These are not the prayers of someone who feels confident in the natural world, as most of us feel confident.

We turn now to another type of material: the many stories of friendships between saints and animals. We must of course realise that there is nothing exclusively Celtic in these stories: we meet similar ones in the Franciscan tradition, in the Russian account of Seraphim of Sarov, and no doubt there are many more. Reading them may add a certain softening to the rough-and-tough impression given by some of the early Irish. You would never suspect, reading the surviving writings of Columbanus, for example, that he had an affectionate side to his character. Although he was normally very astringent, when he thought he was going to be deported back to Ireland, Columbanus wrote an affectionate letter to the community of his monks he thought he would not see again. His hagiographer, Jonas, who wrote shortly after his death, tells us that one of Columbanus's disciples 'said that he had often seen him call the little animal, which men commonly name a squirrel, from the tops of high trees and take it in his hand and put it on his neck and let it go into and come out from his bosom'.[11] There doesn't seem to be any explanation for this except genuine affection. But with other stories of saints and animals we are warned not to take them too superficially. There could be more than love of nature here, there may well be theological motifs. The story of St Cuthbert and the otters offers a good example.[12] Cuthbert was at Coldingham monastery. Every night he disappeared after evening prayer and returned for morning prayer. One of the monks decided to spy on him. So he followed St Cuthbert down to the beach, hid and watched while the saint prayed in and out of the sea all night. But at dawn the saint came up on to the beach with two sea-otters, which played round him, received his blessing, and went back into the sea. The spying monk was terrified and had to be reassured by Cuthbert himself. But why was he afraid? Sister Benedicta Ward, in her treatment of this story, recalls the biblical background: the monk would have known that God had created an original harmony, that the fall of man had destroyed relationships, including that between humans and animals, but that Christ, in the coming kingdom would restore everything. She writes: 'The monk had not been watching a man on the beach with his pets; he had seen the face of Christ in a man so transfigured in prayer that the right order of creation was in him restored.'[13] No wonder the monk was terrified: he had sacrilegiously spied on the kingdom of God, working its powers through Cuthbert in advance of its final fulfilment. If the animal stories in general can be interpreted in the same way it is clear that here too 'nature' is dominated by the biblical understanding of the plan of God for creation.

Did these early Irish then never look upon 'nature' as something in itself, to be studied and admired? It may be that they never did do quite that. But there is one very interesting piece of writing from seventh-century Ireland. This is a theological tract which for a while was attributed to St Augustine of Hippo, and since the author's name is unknown, it is often called Pseudo-Augustine or the Irish Augustine. This little book is called *On the Miracles of Holy Scripture*.[14] He takes utterly seriously God's judgement on his creation on the sixth day that it was 'very good' and he takes that to mean perfect. There cannot therefore be anything new: no new species, no changes which would violate the nature of what has been created. All miracles must then be developments, or revelations of potential already present in the created things, even if the time sequence is speeded up. The obvious example is the changing of water into wine, since in any case wine comes from the water taken in by the vine. But some of the Irish Augustine's examples are more bizarre than that. A recent editor of his work, John Carey, comments: 'his fundamental concerns deserve our attention and respect. Particularly impressive, and as far as I know unparalleled in the early Christian West, is his vision of nature as a harmonious whole whose integrity not even God will violate: I do not think that it is farfetched to see here the early foreshadowing, tentative and isolated, of an ecological sensibility.' So there we are: there was ecology in the early medieval world and it was the Irish who got there first.

There are many other aspects to this subject. For instance, in her book *Celtic Christianity and Nature*, Mary Low has traced how pagan ideas about nature and pagan practices were carried through, and sometimes transformed, in Christian culture. She has chapters on mountains, water, trees, birds and so on, and many fascinating examples of such continuances. The several good translations available of the early Irish poets allow for detailed examination of the early Irish poetic tradition.[15] It seems to me that if I were to summarise how God's glory might be revealed in the Irish tradition, I would want to look principally at the lives and achievements of the early monks. In other words, if we have to make a distinction, we have to look to the realms of history rather than nature. If I had to choose one word to describe what I think I see in these early monks it would be single-mindedness or possibly whole-heartedness – a determination always to put God first. It need not be a ferocious virtue; it apparently was not in our St Aidan. But it was immensely impressive and I am glad that I have had the chance to admire it from afar, and glad indeed to have had the chance to live in a place where it was practised.

Notes

1 On this subject see also Mary Low, *Celtic Christianity and Nature* (Edinburgh: Edinburgh University Press, 1996); Thomas O'Loughlin,

Journeys on the Edges (London: Darton, Longman and Todd, 2000); O'Loughlin, *Celtic Theology* (London: Continuum, 2000); James P. Mackey, *An Introduction to Celtic Christianity* (Edinburgh: T & T Clark, 1995); Oliver Davies and Fiona Bowie, *Celtic Christian Spirituality* (London: SPCK, 1995); Davies (ed.) *Celtic Spirituality: Classics of Western Spirituality* (New York: Paulist Press, 2000).

2 G. S. M. Walker, *Sancti Columbani Opera* (Dublin: Dublin Institute for Advanced Studies, 1970), p. 65.

3 Bede, *Life of St Cuthbert* in B. Colgrave (ed.), *Two Lives of St Cuthbert* (Cambridge: Cambridge University Press, 1940), p. 217.

4 Bede, *Ecclesiastical History of the English People*, B. Colgrave and R. A. B. Mynors (eds) (Oxford: Clarendon Press, 1969), p. 343.

5 For a translation of the text of this poem, see *Iona: The Earliest Poetry of a Celtic Monastery*, T. O. Clancy and G. Markus (eds) (Edinburgh: Edinburgh University Press, 1995), pp. 45–53.

6 ibid., p. 68.

7 Robin Flower, *Poems and Translations* (London: Constable, 1931), p. 116.

8 Alexander Carmichael, *Carmina Gadelica: Hymns and Incantations* (London: Constable, 1900). This was a collection of traditional material made in the nineteenth century from the Hebrides and Western Highlands.

9 For example, no. 159 in *The New English Hymnal*. This is the translation by Mrs C. F. Alexander.

10 There are examples of 'breastplate prayers' in most collections of Celtic prayer. See, for example, Martin Reith, *God in our Midst* (London: SPCK, 1975), nos 35, 36, 38.

11 Jonas, *Life of St Columban*, tr. D. C. Munro, reprint (Felinfach: Llanerch, 1993), p. 52.

12 Bede, *Life of St Cuthbert*, ch. 10.

13 Sr Benedicta Ward, 'The Spirituality of St Cuthbert' in G. Bonner, C. Stancliffe and D. Rollason, *St Cuthbert, his Cult and his Community to* AD *1200* (Woodbridge: Boydell, 1989), p. 72.

14 See the part translation in J. Carey, *King of Mysteries* (Dublin: Four Courts Press, 1998), pp. 51–74.

15 See, for example, *Early Irish Lyrics: Eighth to Twelfth Century*, edited with translation, notes and glossary by Gerard Murphy; with a new foreword by Tomás Ó Cathasaigh (Dublin: Four Courts Press, 1998); D. Greene and F. O'Connor, *A Golden Treasury of Irish Poetry:* AD *600–1200*, reprint (Dingle: Brandon, 1990).

7 The Glory of God Revealed in Humanity

John Gaskell

Over the last few months papers have appeared from time to time in preparation for this grand occasion which I have enjoyed and I hope you have done so too and not only been enjoying it but edified and encouraged by it. One promised item has said 'John Gaskell, the glory of God revealed in humanity'. So I thought that I might approach this lecture with a sort of 'Kit and the Widow' approach. 'Well, I'm the glory of God revealed in humanity, any questions?' And then it struck me that *actually* that is the plan of the fourth gospel. It also struck me that we ought to be able to explain to other men and women when we talk about Catholic and Christian faith that we do in some way or other in humanity share the glory of God and about that I am going to talk today.

This conference has been a very curious experience for me in many ways because in it we have recapitulated my upbringing. In the 1930s, on summer afternoons and spring afternoons too, my father would take me and my brother Desmond, who is a couple of years younger, for walks. We'd walk down the street and then go along Colindeep Lane, which still has hedges beside it, and we'd look for dandelions and daisies. We'd notice stinging nettles which had docks nearby and father would explain perhaps a certain amount about the bees and the birds at the level at which you address boys of perhaps nine and seven. We would be encouraged to pick flowers and learn about the joy of taking home a gift to mother and grandma. We'd go over the bridge across what was then called the Edgware and Morden line and along the paths beside the aerodrome and then up Greyhound Hill. At the top of

Greyhound Hill – this was a new suburb I'm speaking of – there was still a farm and I remember feeling as a little boy frightened by the cows and feeling how alien agriculture – although I didn't know the word – was to nice middle-class people going for a Sunday afternoon walk. We would look out over the great vale towards Harrow where for centuries some of the best wheat in England had been grown, all that was there by then was *houses*. Greyhound Hill, up which we had laboured, and it was a labour indeed – it was a steep hill – went up between grand houses which covered the meadows where, until only 20 years before, the hay for London's cab horses and dray horses had been grown and which meant that transport could go about all over London. My father used to talk about this. And then we went into the churchyard and we'd read the gravestones. There was a pathetic grave of a boy called Desmond, which was my brother's name. That was an opportunity, as I now realise, for a little psychological bullying on my part! My father would talk to us about death and being dead. When you're dead, you're dead, and there's no afterlife. Then we would go round and we would venerate the grave of Sir Stamford Raffles, the founder of Singapore, and my father would talk to us about the benefits of British rule and the King Emperor and the way in which the darkness of heathens had been enlightened by Western insights.

We went into the church, an old country church enlarged because of suburbia needing more seats and more altars. The font at Hendon is a wonderful Norman font – curved arches. My father would explain, 'Wonderful work they did in the Middle Ages and *it's all a mistake.*' I was very poignantly reminded when we were going around the cathedral with Fr Victor Stock – who actually conducted his funeral in due course – of my father taking us round Winchester, Chichester and Canterbury and explaining: 'This is Decorated, this is Early English, it's wonderful engineering; the monks founded law, agriculture; they were the backbone of social life; yet Christianity is man's greatest dream, our biggest mistake.' So we had walks with father, two little unbaptised boys who had a couple of parents who were devoted to encouraging us to think, to value the world and our humanity and our history but to understand quite clearly that God does not exist and the spirit world is a dream. If it sounds a rather didactic childhood it did also include Blackpool Tower and the young John Gielgud as Richard II.

Father would very occasionally talk about the Great War in which he participated because before that he'd been in the army under King Edward VII. He didn't talk about it much; he had a row of medals, decorations, but when the conflict with me came later on about being baptised one of the proofs that God did not exist was 1914–18 and the Cenotaph. So I've gone through all that. In a way I felt just like a little boy being taken around by Victor and listening to the lecturers because our programme has been so much on themes that have illuminated my life right up to the present time. They were sketched out during some children's walks with father.

I want to contrast that – because we're supposed to talk about the glory of God in humanity – with coming out of my front door now and walking to Oxford Street on a wet, hot day or a cold, miserable day. Tens of thousands of people are clamouring past, can't get to the shops quickly enough to spend their money. As they go they eat. In a world in which people are dying of hunger by the thousands day by day they go along eating in a sort of perpetual childhood; we go along drinking from straws even though we are sixty-five. The young clerical workers arrive in the morning carrying their beakers as if they were still four or waiting to be eighty. And if they're not eating, they're chewing because they can't bear not to think we are not eating all the time. They go along in isolation, plugged in to sound; they come out of a cyber world into Oxford Street and they don't even look in the shop windows. I don't feel very much sense of the glory of God in humanity then. I think rather of the prophet Malachi saying that God is going to come and smite the land. Why shouldn't he, it's so hideous!

At the end of the street you find two policemen trying to get rid of a man who has been sleeping in a doorway. As you glance down – the man looks wizened and red-faced – it's just, 'Jesus falls for the first time' in the stations of the cross. And one realises that when Jesus fell for the first time in the stations of the cross probably lots of people didn't take any notice. And the glory of God in humanity is such that in the local authority under which I live it is the policy to clear the beggars from the streets so they won't disturb the tourists. They forget the story of Dives and Lazarus, or possibly even the legend of Martin where the beggar is Jesus himself.

I've chosen those horrors of the day in order not to talk about some of the other things which must fill us with such terrible sorrow.

As you can see I'm a rather curmudgeonly sort of figure and I want to talk to you about three books about curmudgeonly figures because one of the things I want to do is to give you things you can put down in your Christmas shopping list for yourselves or others which will help you understand more of what you do already understand. I'm just here to spur your understanding.

The glory of God. One of the things to hold in our minds throughout this talk which is better than my talk is some words of St Irenaeus, a third-century Bishop of Lyons. These words are written on the Canterbury memorial to Michael Ramsey, who is a sort of patron saint of Affirming Catholicism. These words of Irenaeus, remember them: 'The glory of God is the living man and the life of man is the vision of God.' I'm not clever enough to know but I suspect that a better translation might be 'The glory of God is living man and the life of man is the vision of God.' We heard yesterday about the millions of years that have led up to mankind, one of the things my father knew about and helped make us understand that Genesis is not true. We went to the Natural History Museum to learn that as well of course. But the glory of God is living man. God's purpose in bringing in creation is to bring about living man and, at the heart of it Jesus on the cross, bearing the burden of God and the burden of humanity.

There's a French author who you can still buy in French very easily and in English quite easily, still in print, called François Mauriac. For those who like such things he lived from 1885–1969. He wrote in 1932 a book which is his masterpiece I suppose. In French it's called *Le noeud de vipères*, which you can translate in English as *Knot of Vipers*. And it's the story of a grumpy old man. He belongs to a prosperous, Bordeaux family; he's avaricious, he's filled with hatred yet the book is worth reading because as you read it you see that it's actually a novel about the struggle between the fall in a human being and the grace of God. You can read it as a psychological drama without any Christianity but if you come to it with the eye of faith you can see it's about this man in his struggle with his family and his self drawing near to divine love. His hatefulness is trying to keep at bay what he knows is trying to embrace him. And right at the end of the narrative as he dies he is touched by divine light. As he writes, recording his departure – he doesn't know it's going to be his departure of course – he has suddenly recognised the divine name. But I found that when I read it – I suppose in 1948 or 49 – an enormous revelation came to me that God works with us in our lives. I do recommend Mauriac to you very strongly because he takes seriously the idea of divine providence, of grace, which is a word which hasn't been heard much in our conference I think, and allows God to be one of the actors in his novels.

One of his books is called *The Frontenac Mystery*. The mystery is the 'mystère', the family feeling of the Frontenac family. Again they are prosperous people down in the south west of France and the family is very respectable, but it's got a very rich and successful uncle who's not quite straight-forwardly 'Catholically' proper. He has a mistress housekeeper. I'm going to read to you. (I hope you don't mind these readings. I thought it would be rather much but when I saw those dim slides the other day and heard that wonderful quotation from *Palestrina* I realised that I was going to do these readings whether you liked them or not!) Uncle Frontenac, very prosperous, Bordeaux, formally Catholic man is dying. The family, decent family, loving family who know about him and care for him and care about him and have shared his secret and kept it are about the bed. His mistress housekeeper is comforting him as he is beginning to depart and he is beginning to embark on the final moments of his life. I'm not going to try and explain who all the people are who are being referred to but the point is that the nice family, the loving family who have kept the secret are about the bed and there is the mistress housekeeper beside him.

> 'Are Marie and Danièle here? They will have been in the house of my mistress. I shall have been the cause of their seeing the woman whom I keep. If Blanche and Michel could have known that, they would have cursed me. I have brought Michel's children into the house of my mistress!'
>
> That was all he said. His nose had a pinched look: his face was blue. Raucous sounds came from him, that terrible noise of gurgling which means the end . . . Joséfa, her eyes streaming with tears, took him in her arms, while the Frontenacs withdrew in terror towards the door.
>
> 'You don't need to feel ashamed with them, ducky . . . they're good, they are, they know about things, they understand . . . What is it? . . . what do you want, my poor chickabiddy?'
>
> In sudden panic she turned towards the children:
>
> 'What is he saying? I can't make out what he's saying!'
>
> They could see only too well what that movement of his arm from left to right meant, it meant 'Go away!' God would not let her understand that he was dismissing her, his companion of so many years, his only friend, his servant and his wife.
>
> In the darkness, the noise of the last train smothered her groans.[1]

'But God would not let her understand.' Whereas, of course, holy church said that she was his mistress and the best thing she could do was to pack up and get going *but God would not let her understand.*

Now I think it's very important to cherish the conviction that God is working his purpose out as year succeeds to year (as we used to sing in the school hall with such enthusiasm) and that means in peoples' lives. And a lot of evangelism consists in helping people to understand where their Christianity is and the bits of Catholic glory, the glory of God, which is shining out in them already.

My mother wholly supported the ideas of my father and shared them. When a church warden who was a friend of ours said once during a conversation about what are the children going to do when they grow up – we were all about twelve at the time, a number of girls and boys in the drawing room – and the friend said 'I think John will be a clergyman', my mother said, 'Over my dead body.' We had a terrible tussle about being baptised.

She spent her last months in the clergy house of St Alban's, Holborn, sleeping in the room which had been the bedroom of the sainted Father Mackonochie. She was active right until the end of her life, she died simply from being old. And she would go along Butterfield's wonderful ironwork railing from her bedroom into the drawing room which was also on the first floor. Remember, here's a life-long rationalist unbeliever. And I once said to mother, 'It's very trying for you, darling, it really is trying for you. How do you do it?' She said 'I think about our redeemer on the way to Golgotha.' Diaghilev once said to Jean Cocteau 'Étonnez moi' ('Astonish me') and here's a woman who at the end of her life can say when she's nearly ninety-two the most astonishing thing she's ever said to her son in the whole of his lifetime: 'I think about our redeemer on the way to Golgotha.' Think about the vocabulary. Now how can we know about the interior life of a person who says that in her last months, an unbeliever who has always been near the church? She occasionally went with my father to services to which I invited them (they always came) and at my ordination, which was, of course, conducted by an evangelical bishop, her only comment was, 'There wasn't any incense, dear!'

What I'm talking about is 'Christ in you, the hope of glory' and Christ may be working without our knowing in you, in us, in other people we have to deal with. And we have to bear our witness and tell our truth and commend them hopefully to God because the glory of God is revealed but it is also, a great deal of the time, concealed. But God can see it.

Now not all of you may have heard of François Mauriac who illuminated a great deal of my twenties as I was working up to the idea of being ordained. I probably read his books sitting on the Bakerloo line wearing a bowler hat. But you've all heard of Iris Murdoch. And Iris Murdoch tells us what life's like. People say sometimes about Iris Murdoch's books that 'life's nothing like that, is it?' And I say 'Well, mine is!'

She's got a wonderful book about a very nasty, grumpy,

old man – he is very nasty, a man named Charles Arrowby – called *The Sea, The Sea*; it won the Booker Prize in 1978. Get a second-hand copy, buy a second one and give it to a friend; it's a wonderful tale of obsession. Tiresome old Charles Arrowby is a former theatre director – one of those people from *the theatah* who never quite recognise what goes on in the rest of the world – and he has retired to the seaside and there to his amazement discovers dwelling the woman whom he had really loved right at the beginning of his career but to whom he had not been married. And he very foolishly, cruelly and obsessively tries to pursue her again, particularly when he realises that she is unhappily married. And he is a really terrible person and yet in the middle of this book there's a most extraordinary vision when Arrowby is sitting by the sea wondering how to handle everything and – let's face it – get his own way to the ruin of the happiness of other people of course. He falls into a sort of trance and Iris Murdoch gives us one of her big nature passages. You can see her saying, 'Now what am I going to do now? I think we'll have a bit of fine writing.' In this case I am so impressed that out of Iris Murdoch's grand imagination came this enormous passage of revelation.

He's lying by the sea gazing up into the sky and thinking about how things are going to work out, how's he's going to get his own way:

> [I was] looking straight out at the horizon, where the moon was making an almost but not quite motionless rift of silver. The first stars were already sharp and bright. More stars were coming, more, more. Lying on my back, wrapped in my rug, my hands clasped in front of me, I prayed that all might be well between me and Hartley, that somehow that lifelong faithful remembering, what I now thought of as my mystical marriage, might not be lost or wasted, but somehow come to good! And then, as if the spirit that I had prayed to had admonished me in reply, I tried to put myself out of the picture and to pray only for Hartley: that she might be happy, that Titus might come home, that her husband might love her and she him . . .
>
> Then I found that I was not thinking about Hartley any more . . . I was keeping my eyes open, or trying to, only they kept closing, because I wanted to go on watching the stars,

where the most extraordinary things were happening. A bright satellite, a manmade star, very slowly and somehow carefully crossed the sky in a great arc, from one side to the other, a close arc, one knew it was not far away, a friendly satellite slowly going about its business round and round the globe. And then, much much farther away, stars were quietly shooting and tumbling and disappearing, silently falling and being extinguished, lost utterly silent falling stars, falling from nowhere to nowhere into an unimaginable extinction. How many of them there were, as if the heavens were crumbling at last and being dismantled . . .

[And] now I was looking into the vast interior of the universe, as if the universe were quietly turning itself inside out. Stars behind stars and stars behind stars behind stars until there was nothing between them, nothing beyond them, but dusty dim gold of stars and no space and no light but stars . . . All was movement, all was change, and somehow this was visible and yet unimaginable. And I was no longer I but something pinned down as an atom, an atom of an atom, a necessary captive spectator, a tiny mirror into which it was all indifferently beamed, as it motionlessly seethed and boiled, gold behind gold behind gold.[2]

When we think about humanity as the glory of God we're thinking about the way in which we can have perceptions and experiences and encounters like that and we thank God for them and find them God-given. And I suppose the important thing for us as Catholic Christians is to recognise that the prompting for that recognition is the life and death and resurrection of Jesus and, in particular, his dying and his rising. Quite often, I think, when we talk about the incarnation people think we are talking about smiling babies in cribs and we are actually meaning our redeemer on the path to Golgotha, we are thinking of the first fall on the way to the cross; we are thinking about what we heard about last night in our meditation together and what we also perceive without hearing it. And as we gaze up into the sky we say to ourselves, yes, here is he who bears his glory, has come to us in our sacrament and is to be found in our life and our experiences. I think it's so important to explain to unchristian people that we're not supposed to be having religious experiences all the time in which, as it were, altar bells ring and St so-and-so appears waving in the sky. It's not that. It's about the glory of our lives.

And that brings me to a final curmudgeonly person and that is in a novel published in only 2000 by HarperCollins, readily available in bookshops. The author's name is Salley Vickers and the name of the book is *Miss Garnet's Angel*.

Miss Garnet is a tiresome old lady, well she's not old really, she's younger than me and she has been a bad school-teacher, unpopular, an unkind, strict conveyer of uninteresting information, I suspect. And she and a friend – who she found by advertisement – have had a flat together. When they retire it's not quite clear what they're going to do and just after they retire, in the way it happens to people, the other occupant dies. Then somebody says to Miss Garnet, this rather dry person – she is a communist and an atheist, in our own lifetime, can you imagine? – 'What are you going to do now?' and she suddenly says out of the blue 'I'm going to Venice.' So she goes to Venice and hires a flat.

Her whole life is changed by the experience. She gets to know some nice children and likes them; she falls in love with an elderly man; she meets some very nice young artists whom she assumes are brother and sister but, in fact, they're not. And one day when she is looking out of the window she sees the angel Raphael on the neighbouring roof. Salley Vickers does this in such a matter-of-fact way, that the general experience that we don't see angels out of the window doesn't matter. Miss Garnet did. And any of you who have been involved in the sacred ministry will know that we are constantly meeting people who have!

After she's been settled a bit in the flat, she walks through the back streets of Venice to the Rialto bridge, which is the bridge over the Grand Canal which has shops on it – we have all seen pictures of it and many of you will have been on it. She looks down the Canal – sunshine and domes and the movement and the flickering of the water, all very hypnotic stuff – and says, 'Lord, Lord' and then she says 'why did I say that, why say "Lord, Lord"?' And it's the beginning of the most fascinating story. She goes on and she arrives in St Mark's and she goes to Vespers and she likes the Vespers – the movement, the music, the incense, the crowds, the rather threatening, unpleasant building. That's the beginning but then something more profound happens. The next day or thereabouts, she goes to St Mark's again. I'm going to read this passage because I think it's very important for us because it's about sitting still and being quiet and letting the space speak to you of the eternal spaces and the spaces beyond the eternal spaces that we can get into by being here now and enjoying the glory of the moment.

> The following morning Julia Garnet, this time with [her guide-book] in the pocket of her tweed coat . . . returned to the basilica of St Mark. She entered not by the main door but by a less frequented doorway on the north side. It did not deter her that this side-slip into the cathedral was marked *'Per Pregare'* – 'For Prayer'.
>
> Inside, by long, hanging red and silver lamps, a door was open onto a side chapel. With no special thought in her mind she entered.
>
> About a dozen people sat, in the vaulted, ancient-looking surroundings, listening to a priest reading from a leather book. Julia Garnet looked around. At one end of the chapel a blue mosaic of a huge Madonna gazed down; at the other, a tomb on which rested an inclined marmoreal figure observed by an angel. Twelve candles burned on the table before the tomb.
>
> The priest came to the end of his reading and sat down. There was a pause during which Julia Garnet waited for something to happen. After a while it became apparent that nothing was going to happen, except the silence.
>
> Her first response was annoyance. The Vespers in St Mark's the day before had been dramatic: the flute voices of the clerics, the melodic bells, the incense, the enthralling rhythmic passing and return of the litany-chant thrown between priest and congregation – compared with the threnodic splendour of all that, this abrupt nothingness felt like a cheat. But after a while she began to enjoy the silence. She looked round at the mosaics which seemed to depict some awful martyrdom – certainly there was a body and a tomb and, yes, surely that was the same body being removed from the tomb, and here how eagerly it was being hauled away. There was a kind of ebullience in the

narrative which she made out on the chapel walls as if the dead man had, if not enjoyed, at least participated energetically in his own persecution.

She twisted her neck to look back at the blue Madonna and found a man in a serge suit staring beadily at her, as if his was the task of checking her credentials to be present at the ceremony and was hopeful of finding them wanting. Abashed, she turned from the Madonna to examine the other attenders.

All were women and one, two, three, four, five, six – no seven of them in furs. Now there was a thing! Feeling in the pocket of her own tweed she remembered Vera's letter and almost she started to laugh. What would Vera make of her sitting here in church among seven furs? And which would Vera abhor most? The chapel or the wealth? All the furs were elderly save one: a woman with a long daffodil pony-tail and high gold heels. 'Tarty', Harriet would have called her. (Vera very likely would not have known how to use the word.) But Mary Magdalene had been a tart, hadn't she? thought Julia Garnet . . .

One of the silent furred ones was wearing a wide-brimmed emerald hat. The woman was no younger than herself and Julia Garnet found she wanted just such a hat too. But surely this was not what the silence was for? Designing a wardrobe! Gently, like dripping honey, the quiet filled her pores, comforting as the dreamless sleeps she had fallen prey to. The angel over the inclining man gestured at the heavens; beneath him, another angel on the tomb looked with all-seeing, sightless eyes toward the angels on the holy-water stoup . . . I see an Innumerable company of the Heavenly host crying, 'Holy, Holy, Holy!' . . . The silence was holy. What did 'holy' mean? Did it mean the chance to be whole again? But when had one ever been whole? Silently, silently the priest sat and in the nameless peace Julia Garnet sat too, thinking no thoughts.[3]

Get the book. It's about the way in which God changes us through our experience if we allow ourselves to be changed. We discover how wonderful we are and that, of course, must consecrate us to making sure that other people have things as wonderful as we do. It is all about letting the weight of glory overwhelm us so that we value our humanity and are prepared to serve it as Jesus was prepared to die for it.

Here's a little poem by John Betjeman. I read John Betjeman's letters as my Lent book this year. It's fun to have a lovely book and it was the two volume edition of Betjeman's letters, edited by his daughter; it's a wonderful book. Reading it you go along, it's just about ordinary life, a man making a living, and how the children are getting on and what's going on at the local church, and how the publishing business is going on and then suddenly a holy thought – about Jesus, or communion or the last judgement. And here's a poem about how wonderful we all are, by John Betjeman. It was published in 1945, written a few years before, and it's 'In a Bath Teashop':

> 'Let us not speak, for the love we bear one another –
>   Let us hold hands and look.'
> She, such a very ordinary little woman;
>   He, such a thumping crook;
> But both, for a moment, little lower than the angels
>   In the teashop's ingle-nook.[4]

There we are with our sacramental vision of humanity. We learn it at the altar, we are given it at the font and its face is before us if we look. 'Let us hold hands and look.' We look at the holy face of Jesus, we look at the holy faces of those we love and recognise what is our destiny.

Notes

1 François Mauriac, *The Frontenac Mystery*, tr. Gerard Hopkins (London: Eyre and Spottiswood, 1951), p. 166.
2 Iris Murdoch, *The Sea, The Sea* (London: Triad Granada, 1982), pp. 144–6.
3 Salley Vickers, *Miss Garnet's Angel* (London: HarperCollins, 2000), pp. 31–4.
4 John Betjeman, 'In a Bath Teashop' in *Collected Poems* (London: John Murray, 1958), p. 121.

Epilogue:
The Glory of God Visible and Invisible

Mark Oakley

> Out of his spacious, sacred splendour
> They pried God and forced
> Him into their time;
> And they surrounded and hymned him
> So that he all but disappeared
> Into their darkness.
>
> (Rainer Maria Rilke)

Many spiritual journeys are made in which the believer gradually moves away from thinking that God reveals himself fully, shows himself in all his sacred totality (in Bible, tradition, experience or whatever), to believing that God does not so much *show* himself as *hint* to us, tantalising us with loving but often frustrating intimations. Those who criticise such journeys, defending God's revelation as having a perfectly intelligible precision, are to be found in many of our pulpits at the moment. Those of us, however, who believe in the hinting God continue to resist their seductions of quick clarity and the easy answer, for their exaggerations give them away. There is something not quite right, something inauthentic even, about being told that God can be easily understood if only we listen to the right person or look in the right place. Such a clinging to text or tradition can end up being more of a claim for the inerrancy of our own spirituality rather than being a defence of God's holiness.

Instead it seems true to the tradition of faith, and to our contemporary experience, to say that God's glory is indeed very compelling to many of us. It can even, we believe, be glimpsed from time to time (in God's body language we know as Jesus Christ, for instance) and remains the Lover in a flickering and faltering communion. Nevertheless, God's hidden glory remains gloriously hidden. The silence and ambiguities of God may test our patience but they educate us too: 'You do not have to sit in the dark. If, however, you want to look at the stars, you will find that darkness is necessary.'[1]

A church under pressure is a church that is likely to sell itself short. 'Praise the Lord and pass the ammunition' may have been Dixie Chicks' solution to life-survival in 'Sin Wagon', but it isn't going to do us any favours. It seems to me that we need today to acknowledge again what it is we love and are drawn to as church, namely the reality and freshness of God as mystery, and that to reclaim the truth of God's hidden and transcendent *mystery* will also need careful interpretation at a time when the word more usually translates as 'problem' or 'uncertainty'. How does a world that is now used to calling up facts on a screen in seconds learn about the slow, yet deeper, communication of wisdom? How will hearts used to being jumpstarted at Starbuck's begin to understand what 'conversion of life' might entail? The problem is not just impatience. Where there is a quiet sense of regret that the church just doesn't work for us anymore it is by and large because the language it uses, as well as some of the ideas it conveys, let us down. This has been noticed well before now, of course, but so often the remedy has been sought by trying to make religious language and the words of worship *relevant*. Instead, I would want to argue that the languages of faith should not so much be relevant as *resonant* – if we can see a distinction.

Resonance touches us at a deeper level of understanding, it does not so much answer a need, impose closure, tie things cosily together, as recognise the need and push us, sometimes with discomfort, further into the exploration. A columnist seeks relevance in what she writes. A poet seeks resonance. Resonance is constantly engaged in what Martin Amis has called, 'the war against cliché'. Our society at the moment has a suspicion of authoritative language but, in its desire for relief from its addiction to novelty, is searching for those words that we might just be prepared to die for. In his cell Bonhoeffer thought our most important prayer was that for a language that could reverberate and sound fresh, one layered with comfort and challenge, enabling recognitions only as the words are spoken. We are still praying.

In 63 BC the Romans stormed the Jerusalem Temple and were, we are told, astonished to find the Holy of Holies empty, with no statues and no object of worship. This shock of absence, I believe, lies forever at the heart of faith in God. *'The sensation of silence'*, wrote John Updike, 'cannot be helped: a loud and evident God would be a bully, an insecure tyrant, an all-crushing datum instead of, as he is, a bottomless encouragement to our faltering and frightened being.'[2] It is true that as we try to articulate God we discover his elusiveness, his receding before us. God gives us just enough to seek him, and never enough to find him fully. To do more would inhibit our freedom that is so dear to him. 'Such a fast God', says R. S. Thomas, 'always before us and leaving as we arrive.' We relate to God only in the context of nearness and distance for if we ever think we possess him we will stop desiring him. It is as if we know there is a God because he keeps disappearing. Our longing is the necessary constant. Desire is the heartbeat of faith. Faith is a love of the hidden, a pursuit in relationship, a search for the visibility of the invisible. 'We want God's voice to be clear but it is not. It is as deep as night, with a dark clarity, like an x-ray. It reaches our bones.'[3]

Our concern to *resolve* the mystery of God is corrected into a desire to *deepen* it. For this reason I believe people of faith should be unapologetically poetic, poetic in the will to capture truth but to resist closure. Theology, like a poem, is never finished, it can only be abandoned. In the words of Octavio Paz, poetry is 'memory become image and image become voice'. Those of us in the churches need to cultivate the poetry, the metaphor, symbol and myth of our tradition, and be unashamed in disappointing those who want our religion to be a *source of facts* about God, the universe and everything. Such 'easy religion' will always let you down in the end. 'Our religion has materialised itself in the fact', wrote Matthew Arnold, 'in the supposed fact; it has attached its emotion to the fact, and now the fact is failing it . . . the strongest part of religion today is its unconscious poetry'. I would suggest that we need *intimation* as well as *specification*, a language of possibility, a vocabulary for those who don't quite believe their disbelief. If, in the postmodern, knowledge exists no longer in narrative form but in the form of information, bringing a loss of meaning, we need to reveal that God, at least, will never be revealed propositionally. No, 'God is like a person who clears his throat while hiding and so gives himself away.'[4]

As I have said, there will be those who find this frustratingly nebulous or worryingly heretical. They are in a good tradition for those early disciples of Jesus, it seems, were equally rattled by what the sacred parables and the secrecy added up to. As the work of Sallie McFague has reminded us:

> a theology that is informed by parables is necessarily a risky and open-ended kind of reflection. It recognises not only the inconclusiveness of all conceptualization when dealing with matters between God and human beings . . . but also the pain and scepticism – the dis-ease – of such reflection. Theology of this sort is not neat and comfortable; but neither is the life with and under God of which it attempts to speak. The parables accept the complexity and ambiguity of life as lived in the world and insist that it is in this world that God makes his gracious presence known. A theology informed by the parables can do no less – and no more.[5]

All this has implications for every level and activity of Christian discipleship, not least in the way we worship, interpret Scripture, preach, speak of our faith to one another, and treat one another as sacraments of the divine mystery. We only love God as much as the person we love least. Part of the worry in the present climate is surely that it is not so much that people will believe nothing as that they will believe anything, and many so called spiritualities on offer are so self-oriented. Christian people have a concept of the self that is, rather, selfless. We in the church should not be reflecting back to the surface of society a way of being and communicating that is simply factual, informative, or deadened with opinions and rhetorical relevance. If God is in this world as poetry is in the poem, then we need poetic assurance, diverse ways of communicating in unified purpose, for truth is not the elimination of ambiguity. And not all those who seek truth by wandering and wondering are necessarily lost. They are just aware that there is still so much to take in.

In her poem 'The Minister', Anne Stevenson asks why we need the minister today at a funeral – to dig the hole, to drive the hearse, to bake the cakes? No. 'We have to have the minister', she says, 'so the words will know where to go. Imagine them circling and circling the confusing cemetery. Imagine them roving the earth without anywhere to rest.'[6] If this is so, if a priest is a sort of 'poet-in-residence' then we need to be clear as to our task and our tools. As that larger than life Australian poet, Les Murray, prays: 'God, at the end of prose, somehow be our poem.' The language of faith, the ways in which we try to give voice to the glory of the sacred in our midst, are akin to the languages of art, where more is communicated than can be understood in a single encounter. It is therefore essential for those of us in the community of Christian faith to take the work of our artists as seriously as our own, to engage in conversations, and to be challenged, provoked and unsettled by much of what they bring with them. As David Brown argues in his chapter in this volume, we engage with the arts not just to seek illustrations for our own ideas but to express and explore further what it is that God might be expressing and exploring. Like theatres, churches might yet still become gymnasiums for human imagination, a place where vision can team up with good judgement, where revelation might be strictly unthinkable but able, against the odds, to transform human hearts.

The arts are engaged in bringing into partial visibility what is invisible. The arts are a language of encounter and journey; they show the way to a land of hints and guesses, they can shock, outrage and resurrect. A church that seeks to serve and relate to the source of life and love, the God of hidden glory, must now be unapologetically poetic and artistic in its life and witness, polyvalent not totalitarian, a large gallery in whose many rooms you can hear people busily and excitedly trying to interpret what is going on in this large sacred picture we call reality. And it might be time to confess that, when it comes to God's glory, shadows point the way.

Notes

1 Annie Dillard, *Teaching a Stone to Talk* (New York: Harper and Row, 1988), p. 31.
2 John Updike, *Self-Consciousness* (New York: Knopf, 1989), p. 229.
3 Ernesto Cardenal, cited in Michael Paul Gallagher, *Dive Deeper: The Human Poetry of Faith* (London: Darton, Longman and Todd, 2001), p. 77.
4 Meister Eckhart, cited in Philip Yancey, *Reaching for the Invisible God* (London: HarperCollins, 2000), p. 116.
5 Sallie McFague, *Speaking in Parables: A Study in Metaphor and Theology* (London: SCM, 1975), p. 7.
6 Anne Stevenson, 'The Minister' in *The Collected Poems 1955–1995* (Oxford: Oxford University Press, 1996), p. 62.

Sermon:
What is Celtic Spirituality?

Brendan O'Malley

The Celts were not given to theological or doctrinal specu-
lation. Their teaching was in the example of the lives they
lived; in their stories, meditations, poetry, art and humour.
Celtic spirituality cannot be fully captured in words – it is
to be experienced and savoured rather than analysed.
Celtic Christians lived in harmony with animals, plants and
all other creatures and practised a way of life very close to
that of the Desert Fathers whose spirituality had likewise
embraced the whole natural order.

At a time when people are searching for a spirituality to
inform the present concern for the wholeness of the individual and of the planet, there is to be found within the tradition of Celtic Christianity a reverence and respect for the
entire created community which, with humankind,
glorifies God. The church in this land is the custodian of
deep spiritual truths and has an established power base
from which it can exert a strong influence on people's
search for the Christ of the incarnation. It therefore needs to
harness the powerful spiritual witness of our Celtic forefathers. It ignores their message at its peril.

Let us for a moment move from wherever we are to
Mount Athos, a peninsula of Greece on the Aegean Sea. On
the holy mountain there was until recent times a certain
hermit, who lived in a high place near the end of the peninsula on the steep slopes about a thousand feet above the
sea, looking out over the waves. A disciple came and
wanted to learn from the old man his way of life. They used
to pray all night saying the Psalms and praying in silence.
But, before they went into the darkness of the chapel with
its lamps lit in front of the Holy Icon, the old hermit would

sit on the balcony, facing out towards the waves, watching
the setting sun, and he required his disciple to sit there too
for about twenty minutes, in silence. After this had hap-
pened several times the disciple said to the old man, 'Why
do we have to go and look at the setting sun every evening,
surely we've looked at this view enough? What are you
doing when you sit there, silently facing the setting sun?'
The old man replied, 'I am gathering fuel.' Looking out
over the beauty of God's creation, he was gathering energy
to sustain him through the vigil of the night.[1] This represents an attitude towards the natural creation that is
very close to certain themes in Celtic spirituality; the God-
centred life of our Celtic forefathers.

The Celtic saints had a deep perception of the immanent
presence of God in all the familiar things in the world about
us. Every well-spring, wood and stone took on a mystical
significance. This is exactly what the hermit of Mount Athos
was aware of. This dwelling in the beauty of God's creation
was not something separate from his nightly prayer but the
two reinforced and complemented each other.

> The Maker of all things,
> The Lord God worship we:
> Heaven white with angels' wings,
> Earth and the white-waved sea.[2]

The Christian is the one who wherever he or she looks, sees
Christ and rejoices in him. As the prayer says, 'Thine own
from thine own, we offer thee.' In everything and for everything we offer Christ; we are to find Christ in everything.
There was a saying circulated among the early Christians
attributed to Christ though not found in the Gospels, 'Lift
the stone and you will find me, cut the wood in two and
there am I.'[3] The Celts' sense of God's presence and power
was so great because they saw God in everything, wor-
shipped him through everything, and turned to him for aid
and guidance for everything.

> I am the wind that breathes upon the sea,
> I am the wave on the ocean,
> I am the murmur of leaves rustling,
> I am the rays of the sun

> I am the beam of the moon and the stars,
> I am the power of trees growing,
> I am the bud breaking into blossom,
> I am the movement of the salmon swimming,
> I am the courage of the wild boar fighting,
> I am the speed of the stag running,
> I am the strength of the ox pulling the plough,
> I am the size of the mighty oak tree,
> And I am the thoughts of all people
> who praise my beauty and grace.[4]

Modern sophistication has paradoxically given us the yearning for simpler times, and to think that Celtic faith just came naturally. 'Weren't they lucky,' we say, 'that they had it to sustain them in their trials?' It was not luck, it was practice. We need to practise the presence of God. It takes a great deal of work simply to train ourselves to turn to God. The Celts taught themselves and their children to turn to God almost constantly.

> As the hand is made for holding and the
> eye for seeing, thou hast fashioned me for joy.
> Share with me the vision that shall find it
> everywhere:
> in the wild violet's beauty;
> in the lark's melody:
> in the face of a steadfast man:
> in a child's smile:
> in a mother's love:
> in the purity of Jesus.[5]

Among the pre-Christian dwellers of this land perhaps it was believed that a god, or gods, was actually present in the wells, in the stone. The seeds of Christianity in Celtic lands had fallen into earth fertilised by centuries of natural worship. The pre-Christians believed in tree gods and water goddesses, in the mountains and animals and sunlight. When combined, the new faith and the old beliefs gave Celtic Christianity a unique flavour.

We Christians today cannot believe in a multiplicity of gods but we still believe in the same indwelling presence. Well-springs are holy places not just by virtue of the fact

that a holy saint lived there and prayed there, but by virtue
of the fact of what they are: living waters springing up from
the earth and the gift of God. That is what makes for a holy
place.

It is perhaps a good thing to remember that the early
Christians recognised that every fountain had its own particular guardian angel who is a symbol of the living embod-
iment of God's presence in that place. They loved all
creatures for what they are. Water, for example, is loved for
itself, not because it is full of sprites and ethereal things but
because it is a creature like us. As a creature, water is our
sister, and it is hardly normal to pour toxic acid into your
sister! We are interrelated with all creation. We not only
pour forth from the hand of God, our Father Creator, but in
common with all of creation are brought forth out of our
Mother, the Earth, by the action of the love of the Father
through the power of the Holy Spirit.

> He breathes through all Creation,
> He is love, eternal love.[6]

We find the hand of God in all things: 'Lords, brethren, and
sisters, be joyful, and keep your faith and belief, and per-
form the little things which you have heard and seen with
me, and I will go the road which our fathers have travelled'
said St David to his disciples.[7] We are to value the little
things and find God in them. David's approach to the life
of the Spirit was centred in the everyday 'little things' we
do as we live our lives:

> It is these little actions which reflect our true attitude both
> towards life and towards those around us. In any community
> small and habitual kindnesses and expressions of respect for
> others ('parch' – that quality which remains all important in
> traditional Welsh rural communities) will provide stability,
> unity and wholeness. Acts of unkindness or apparent contempt
> on the other hand, however trivial, can lead to the total disin-
> tegration of a society as feuds develop and are fuelled by an
> unwillingness to forgive.[8]

The whole approach of Celtic spirituality is familial, simple
and mystical. Mysticism is not merely visions and ecstasy;
Christian mysticism consists in living the Christian mys-

tery and being transformed by it. The mystical approach is to find the extraordinary in the ordinary, to find eternity in the familiar objects that we handle and use every day.

> My Chief of generous heroes, bless
> my loom and all things near to me,
> bless me in all my busy-ness,
> keep me for life safe-dear to thee.[9]

We are to have towards the world round about us a double value; we are to value each thing for its specific vastness or 'is-ness'. We are to become aware that we are in each particular thing and then in each thing and through each thing we are to apprehend the presence of the living God. Things that are solid, with sharp outline and distinct relief, are at the same time transparent sacraments of God's presence, and means of communion with him.

> Teach me, my God and King,
> in all things thee to see;
> and what I do in anything
> to do it as for thee.
> A man that looks on glass,
> on it may stay his eye;
> or, if he pleaseth, through it pass,
> and then the heaven espy.[10]

The whole universe is interrelated and interdependent. All matter is connected, a fact acknowledged by both mystic and scientist. All movement, sound, vibration has a repercussion and effect throughout the whole of the created order. The most important heritage, which Celtic Christianity received from the old religion, was the profound sense of the immanence of God in the world. The Celtic Christians remained very much aware of the divine presence in all nature and it is this sense of an all-pervading presence that is characteristic of their Christian piety. Through prayer these Celts experienced their relationship with the whole creation. Entering into harmony with the universe they journeyed towards the ultimate destiny of God's world. Seeking the Lord of the Elements and journeying through life for the love of God they achieved a state of grace.

Notes

1 Brendan O'Malley, *Celtic Spirituality* (Cardiff: Church in Wales Publications, 1992), p. 4.

2 Early Irish Poem in Brendan O'Malley, *A Celtic Primer* (Norwich: Canterbury Press, 2002), p. 242.

3 Cited in Brendan O'Malley, *A Welsh Pilgrim's Manual,* second impression (Llandysul, Wales: Gomer Press, 1995).

4 This poem is to be found in *The Black Book of Carmarthen,* a Welsh work of great antiquity. Edited by Meirion Pennar, *The Black Book of Carmarthen* (Lampeter: Llanerch Publishers, 1989).

5 Alister Maclean, *Hebridean Altars* (Edinburgh: Moray, 1937).

6 Bishop Timothy Rees in Brendan O'Malley, *A Pilgrim's Manual, St David's* (Marlborough: Paulinus Press, 1985).

7 ibid.

8 Patrick Thomas, *The Opened Door – A Celtic Spirituality* (Brechfa: Silyn Publications, 1990).

9 Translated by A. Carmichael in *Carmina Gadelica* (Edinburgh: Scottish Academic Press, 1972).

10 George Herbert in *The New English Hymnal* (Norwich: Canterbury Press, 1986), no. 456.

Sermon Preached on Holy Cross Day

Jack Nicholls

I would sum up my understanding of the glory of God as revealed in us and through us in the phrase 'What a mess, and yet . . .'. It is certainly a phrase which goes through my mind when I look into a mirror 'what a mess, and yet . . .'.

Religion is powerful and, therefore, dangerous. Although this is not the whole story, nonetheless it is true to say that religious people have too often taken advantage of the power of religion in order to control the lives of others. 'You need salvation', they say. 'We are the only ones who can provide it and we do so on our terms.' The result of this is the enslavement of others under the pretext of bringing them freedom. From this the church needs to repent. 'What a mess, and yet . . .'.

I made my first appearance at the General Synod of the Church of England when I became a diocesan bishop. There was a debate on religious broadcasting and some (many?) speakers bemoaned the fact that there wasn't more overtly religious broadcasting at peak viewing times. My response, had I been called (which I wasn't because I didn't know the system), would have been to remind us that God doesn't need religious broadcasting to get through. Melvyn Bragg's interview with Dennis Potter a few weeks before the latter's death from cancer was shot through with the glory of God, though neither of the participants would claim to be more than sympathetic agnostics. 'What a mess, and yet . . .'. Fortunately glimpses of glory are not dependent on religious intermediaries.

Some time ago there appeared in the *Sunday Times* travel supplement (6 September 1998) the following paragraph:

Even on a good day, the River Ganges picks up levels of faecal coliform bacteria as it flows past Varanasi that are 10,000 times the World Health Organisation's standards for drinking water.

Yet drink the water is precisely what people come here to do. A million Hindus a year, from all over India, make the pilgrimage to this, the most sacred spot on India's most sacred river, to bathe in it and to drink the water.

It's a contradiction that's not easy for the first-time visitor to swallow: that a place of such startling pollution is where people come to be purified. And more than that: that this is one of the only places on earth where *moksha* – liberation from the endless cycle of rebirth – is guaranteed; that here, consumed by traffic fumes and sewage and the stench of rotting animal matter, one should be granted the privilege of breathing one's last. Die in Varanasi, the Hindu texts maintain, and you'll be released, once and for all, from the pain of existence, from the anguish of continual rebirth and death.

For Varanasi is a ford, a *tirtha*, between heaven and earth – one of those unique crossing points where gods and goddesses can descend to this world and mortals can be transferred direct to the afterlife. Die here, in the embrace of Mother Ganga, in Shiva's sacred city, and your spirit will be united with the Absolute, will find its longed-for, eternal, perfect peace.

'What a mess, and yet . . .'.

A similar theme is picked up in the Book of Exodus where the children of Israel, after being attacked by poisonous snakes are healed as they gaze on the bronze image of the same snakes. The bitter waters of Mara are made sweet when Moses throws wood into the water. We have no idea what sort of wood, but the Fathers suggested that it was the very same wood from which the cross was made and so we come to the 'crux' of the matter. 'What a mess, and yet . . .'.

On 27 December in the year 537, the Emperor Justinian stood in the newly completed Church of Holy Wisdom, in Constantinople. The church had taken less than six years to build and has been described in modern times as the finest building in the world. Little wonder then that after a long period of silence Justinian was heard to say, 'Solomon I have surpassed thee.' Yet great as the building was and is, a yet greater Christian treasure was housed inside it; the greatest relic of all, the True Cross. The Cross had already been in Constantinople for over 200 years, having been discovered, so we are told, by St Helena, the mother of the Emperor Constantine, when Helena at the age of seventy-two had become the first documented Christian pilgrim to the Holy Land. Helena was faced with a dilemma in her discovery of the True Cross, when, as might be expected, she discovered three. Which of the three was the True Cross and which were the two crosses of the thieves crucified on either side of our Lord? She solved her problem by placing each of the crosses over the body of a dying woman, the woman was miraculously restored to life and health when the True Cross was placed upon her. The instrument of death had become the instrument of healing.

The place and instrument of death, of pollution, of our worst, is the place of God's best. 'What a mess, and yet . . .'. God continues this work in the human heart where we discover that nothing about us is so perfect that it does not need redemption and nothing about us is beyond redemption. Our all too human heart is the mess where redemption is wrought.

Not long before he died Donald Nicholl wrote in the *Tablet* for Easter 1997:

> Though the advances resulting from the Enlightenment are desirable they are not *crucial* because they do not respond to the *crucial* need of the wounded human condition, which cannot be healed by any achievements of progress, but only by redemption . . . What we have to remember is that in spite of all our failings and our wretchedness it is actually only believers who are actively engaged in the one thing necessary, the task of redemption, which can only happen if there is a change in the human heart.

All this was expressed with great simplicity by St Seraphim of Sarov when he said 'Have peace in your heart and thousands round you will be saved.' The point was proved within himself when, after 30 years of silence and 1000 days and nights of constant prayer, his own heart was purified. He wore the white of Easter always, greeted everyone as 'my joy, Christ is risen' and was himself transfigured so that others saw the light of the glory of God through him. He proved that the presence of one who is pure in heart can change lives. Donald Nicholl says, 'Everything in Seraphim's life, his capacity for joy, for silence, for healing and gentleness, for freedom and peace, and the capacity to serve as a light for others, all come from the risen life which he had embraced.'

We too can participate in glory and others will see glory shining through us, so we ourselves, others and God's whole creation will be transfigured *but* we must begin at the place of glory revealed, where Christ was lifted up. Here sin, pollution, pain and suffering meet with love, judgement and forgiveness and love's redeeming work is done. It is the foot of the cross where we must stand and remain until it is done, accomplished, in us and we can become Easter for all.

I may be a mess, and yet . . .

Appendix:
The Glory of God Revealed on the Cross

A Meditation on the Seven Last Words of Christ from the Cross
Jeffrey John

Introduction by Perran Gay

Jeffrey John's meditation took the form of an extended meditation on the Passion of Christ in St Oswald's Church, Durham on the eve of Holy Cross Day. The addresses were given in the context of a liturgical performance by the Allegri Quartet of the movements of Franz Joseph Haydn's *The Seven Last Words of Christ*. Jeffrey John's addresses were interspersed with the movements of Haydn's music.

Haydn's music was originally scored for full orchestra, and received its first performance at Cadiz Cathedral, where it was used within a similar liturgical context. Haydn later adapted it for string quartet, which was the version (Opus 51) played. It consists of a short Introduction, seven *Adagios* (each one offering a reflection on one of the 'words'), and a concluding *Presto* entitled *Il Terremoto* (The Earthquake) depicting the cataclysmic events that follow the death of Christ in the gospel accounts.

Throughout the Vigil, the blessed sacrament was exposed on the altar as a focus for prayer and adoration, and the service concluded with Benediction.

JEFFREY JOHN

Introduction

Maestoso e adagio

1. Pater, dimitte illis; nonenim sciunt quid faciunt

As they nailed him to the Cross, Jesus prayed, 'Father, forgive them, they know not what they do'.

Father, forgive them, they know not what they do.
Father, forgive us, when we know not what we do.
And forgive us especially when we prefer to keep it that way.

Crucifixion was nothing new, after all. The soldiers were used to the screams and blood and mess. It was their job, they were only obeying orders. That's what they all say down the ages, the soldiers and executioners and torturers and concentration camp guards. 'We were only obeying orders. It was our job.' They steel themselves to it and soon get used to it.

And so, in our way, do we.

So, Father:
forgive us our own indifference in the face of suffering,
our own deliberate lack of imagination,
our wilful shutting out of other people's pain.

Forgive us when we rush past the beggar in the street,
when we flick past the pictures of the starving on the TV
  screen,
when we can't find time and care for the ones who need our
  time and care,
when we can't even be bothered to write the letter or sign the
  petition,
when we close off our compassion because compassion costs
  too much,
and we say like the soldiers hammering you to the cross,
'This is the way the world is, we can't change it.'

When we don't even notice any more as we drive in the nails,
then, Father, forgive us, for we choose to know not what we do.

2. Amen dico tobo; hodie mecum eris in paradiso

The penitent thief prayed 'Lord, remember me when you come into your kingdom.' Jesus answered, 'Truly I tell you, today you shall be with me in paradise.'

It's as easy as that, then! A deathbed conversion, a quick 'I'm sorry', and a lifetime of sin's forgiven, and heaven's guaranteed.

Well, yes … and no.

What is repentance? A relationship restored. It's rarely a matter of a moment; or if it is, it's returning to a love that's already known, if only as possibility. Even the penitent thief had somehow learned to recognise love when he saw it, and had the sense to welcome it. The other was too angry, too blinded, too closed off by failure and pain.

So Lord:

when the crisis comes for me, help me somehow to keep an open heart.

Remind me that love is the only possible heaven, and lovelessness is hell.

Save me from the bitterness that might ever make me shut you out.

Save me from the self-hatred that judges me more harshly than you ever would.

And when the end comes for me, Lord,

help me to stand before you without fear.

Break down the stupid pride or shame that would make me turn away.

Give me courage to see myself in the light of your love,

and so to find real repentance, and my real self, in the paradise of your presence.

3. Mulier, ecce filius tuus, et tu, ecce mater tua

When Jesus saw his mother and the disciple whom he loved standing beside her, he said to his mother, 'Woman behold your son'; and to the disciple 'behold your mother'. And from that day the disciple took her as his own.

'Home is where the heart is' – and the hurt. To paraphrase Philip Larkin, 'They muck you up, your mum and dad.'

For good or ill, our parents largely make us who we are, and we have to live with it. Yet we also say we are born again, we are a new creation, as children of God. And if we are born again, we're also given a new family in which to grow up again – spiritual parents, brothers and sisters and children. What is the church meant to be, but a new network of relationships, visible and invisible, through which we grow into spiritual maturity, and heal the wounds we all inherit from our earthly families?

Lord Jesus,
The gospel tells us you had trouble with your family too.
But by your cross everything we are can be redeemed, reordered and made new.
You gave your mother to the beloved disciple and to us,
to be mother in the new family of all your beloved disciples in your church.
May she protect us and pray for us,
and in the light of your love, and hers,
and the love of all our brothers and sisters in earth and heaven,
help us grow up again as children of the Father,
until we become the people you made us to be.

4. Eli, eli, lama sabachthani?

At the ninth hour Jesus cried with a loud voice, 'Eloi, eloi, lamma sabachthani'; 'My God, My God, Why have you forsaken me?'

What is happening here? Who has forsaken whom? Is this the innocent Son, the sinless substitute, paying the price of our sin to appease the angry Father? Is this God punishing Jesus instead of us, exacting retribution, venting his fury? What kind of God is this that has to be placated with blood? What kind of monster rules the minds of those who fear that the ultimate truth about God is not his love but his wrath?

'I and the Father are one' says Jesus. 'Whoever has seen me has seen the Father.' The very notion of a loving Jesus punished by a wrathful Father is a blasphemy that should be rooted out of the Christian heart and mind. As Paul says, '*God was in Christ*, reconciling the world to himself.' On the cross it is *God* who puts himself in the place of all those with whom he was supposed to be angry. *God* pays the price and takes the consequences of our sin; *God* is hurt for our transgressions and bruised for our iniquities. *God* suffers and bleeds and weeps and dies.

And at the root of it all, the sharpest pain is the pain of our separation from him. This too God himself has had to share; this is his ultimate self-identification with us, the lowest point of his incarnation. The deepest mystery and paradox of our faith is that it is *God* himself who cries 'My God, why have you forsaken me?' He puts himself where we are, so that we might come to be where he is.

> God our Father,
> Help us to know that you are love,
> even when the evidence seems contrary.
> Help us see that you do not will this world's afflictions,
> but have shared them, and still share them, in your Son.
> Help us see that on the cross, as in the crib,
> you are Lord God Immanuel,
> God with us, not against us,
> in Christ our Lord.

5. Sitio

Jesus said 'I thirst.' They offered him wine mingled with myrrh, but he would not drink it.

They offered the drugged wine as an act of kindness, to alleviate the pain as well as the thirst. But he refused it. This thirst is something deeper, and only one can quench it.

As the deer longs for the running streams,
So my soul yearns for you O God.
My heart and my soul are thirsty for God, for the living God.
O when shall I come and see the face of God?

O God, you are God, for you I long;
My soul thirsts for you, my flesh faints for you
Like a dry weary land without water. (Psalm 42)

Lord God,
all our life long we try to slake our thirst for you with other
    things.
We take the drugs of distractions and substitutes for you,
but still the thirst remains.

Sometimes, when you surprise us with your glory,
we realise there's nothing else we really want but you.
Then we forget again and fall away.
But in the end, Lord, when our cross comes,
and everything else has fallen away from us,
we know there will be you and only you.

So keep us thirsty, Lord.
Save us from being satisfied with what is less than you.
Teach us to look for you and find you beyond all other things,
So that when the going's hard, and life turns dry,
we can use this desert valley as a well,
and find it filled with pools of water.

6. Consummatum est

Jesus cried 'It is finished.'

It's finished, it's all over: he's good as dead.

It's finished, it's accomplished: the victory's won.

Which is it, success or failure? The paradox of the cross is that the greatest defeat is simultaneously the greatest victory. But this mystery of gain through loss, strength through weakness, life through death, isn't some distant alchemy done 2000 years ago on the cross. It's real experience. It's the pattern of Christian life for every one of us.

'Take up your cross daily' says Jesus. 'You have to lose your self to find your true self.' Somehow we have to learn to loosen our grip on our selfish self, so that we can find our new and eternal self, given away in love to others and to God. And sometimes – too often – it seems we can only learn the hard way.

'Everything works for good for those who love God' – even the worst things. What may seem the worst disaster in our own sight may be the only thing that can save us in the sight of God. That's why Paul said at the end of his life that despite all his achievements and successes, the only things he will boast of are his weaknesses and failures, because they were the things that made him rely on God's strength, not his own – and cancelled the great I of his ego into a cross:

> *We proclaim Christ crucified, a stumbling block to Jews and folly to Greeks, but to those who are called, both Jews and Greeks, Christ the power of God and the wisdom of God. For God's foolishness is wiser than human wisdom, and God's weakness is stronger than human strength. (1 Cor. 1:23)*

> *Therefore I am content with weaknesses, insults, hardships, persecutions and calamities; for when I am weak, then I am strong. (2 Cor. 12:10)*

JEFFREY JOHN

7. Pater, in manus tuas commendo spiritum meum

Father, into your hands I commend my spirit.

Jesus had hung on the cross for three hours and was clearly going to die, yet John's Gospel presents Jesus' death as an act of will. He 'yields up' his spirit in a final act of faith in the Father.

Clergy and medical staff know very well that patients near to death can sometimes choose to 'hang on' for days or weeks before dying, and when they are ready, they choose to let go of life by an act of mind and spirit. The will can still exercise authority even over a failing body.

What matters is having the trust to let go, the confidence that God is real, and God is love; that he made us for himself, and wills that nothing he has made should be lost. In him we will not be less than we are now, but infinitely more – we shall be our truest selves, as we were made to be. In him we can also expect to regain the loves we thought we had lost, as all things are gathered up, renewed and made perfect in his new creation.

> So, Father:
> make us ready to meet you, whether in this life or in death.
> We commit our way to you, confident of your care for us.
> Though we fail you and fall from you, lead us home at last;
> and give us the faith and trust to say:
> 'Lord, into your hands I commend my spirit.'

Il Terremoto (The Earthquake)

Presto con tutta la forza

© 2004 Jeffrey John